ROCKY BOWERS PARRA

Embracing Mrs. Mommy

Learning from, living with and loving someone with autism

amazon

kdp

kindle direct publishing

First edition

ISBN: 978-0-578-64773-9

Editing by Kate Brown Treick
Cover art by Lindsey Cleworth

This book was professionally typeset on Reedsy.
Find out more at reedsy.com

To Brett, BethAnne, Peyton, Walker and Matthew

Thanks to each of you for your part in helping me become Mrs. Mommy. I love you all "to infinity and beyond."

Contents

Foreword

A Letter to My Much Younger Self

In the midst of a recent bout of decluttering, I found my high school memory book. One of the pages encouraged my high school senior self to predict where she expected to find herself in 5 years and again in 10 years after high school. I laughed as I read the responses of that eighteen-year-old country girl. Then I grew more introspective as I thought about how wildly my life from those predictions and how grateful I am for that, so I decided to write myself a letter.

Dear Eighteen-Year-Old Rocky,

Life doesn't always turn out the way you plan, and it's not always fair, but that's okay. It is actually better than okay; changed plans and life's challenges provide for some of the best surprises and blessings.

You are not going to be the career woman you planned to be. You won't be a lawyer or a journalist, but an accountant and then a stay at home mom! You learned in college that you liked writing for yourself more than for others and that you didn't like to present arguments. In a meeting with your advisor, he suggested you try accounting. You could still graduate in four years and were likely guaranteed a job! You listened and found out that accounting was a great fit. Thirty years later, you still use those skills you learned in accounting in your personal life and as a community volunteer.

You married that guy that was just your best friend all those years ago. He is still your best friend and so much more today. He's practicing medicine just like he thought he would, and that shouldn't surprise you a bit. One of the greatest gifts he will ever give you, besides your kids, was an introduction to Catholicism. You've been Catholic for 27 years now and find so much comfort in your faith. Furthermore, he's an amazing husband and father and still knows just how to push your buttons by cheering for the "wrong" team or taking the opposing side of an argument just because he can. Some things never change!

You have four children, YES, F-O-U-R! Just three more than you planned! Two girls and two boys. You get more enjoyment out of being a mom than you ever imagined! As you face the reality of a slowly-emptying nest, you wish the hands of time would just slow down. You've enjoyed every bit of motherhood, from dirty diapers to packing lunches to listening to The Wiggles for the last twenty years! You experienced the lows and highs of motherhood, infertility, morning sickness, and miscarriage to watching first steps, hearing first words, being a sports mom and room mom, and watching children graduate from high school.

Your last child, the surprise one, changed you to your very core. He came bouncing into the world at 9 pounds and 13 ounces. The older kids adored him and he completed the family.

Around fifteen months, he began to change and regress. You knew something was different with him, but you didn't know what it was or what to call it. Eventually, you learned it was autism.

Autism changed your world. In the beginning, it was incredibly tough, and in many ways still is. My word to you today? Hold on, breathe, pray; it will get better. You will learn, you will grow strong, protective and fierce. Yes, fierce, like a mother warrior. Your other children will be okay—they will be better than okay. They will thrive. They will become kind, independent, strong individuals, and they will love and protect Matthew.

You will write again. You will write about your experience with Matthew and autism. You want others to have an inside view of one family's experience with autism. You will advocate for those who can't or don't know how. You will work to educate everyone in Matthew's world to presume competence in Matthew and others like him.

You will be so grateful that life didn't turn out quite the way you planned in 1988. You will thank God for knowing what you needed when you didn't and for seeing what we can't. Trust me, I know.

Sincerely,

Forty-Nine-Year-Old Rocky
   (Written April 27, 2019)

Preface

Some of you know me as Rocky, some as Mrs. Parra, others still as Brett's wife or BethAnne, Peyton and Walker's mom. Yet unless you follow me on Instagram or are around Matthew and I a lot, you do not know me as Mrs. Mommy.

A couple of years ago, Matthew began calling me Mrs. Mommy. We do not have any idea why. Perhaps he heard it somewhere else first. My theory is that he referred to most of the adult women in his life as "Mrs." or "Ms." and decided Mommy needed that title in front of her name, too! It stuck and he uses it pretty consistently when calling me or referring to me. When he really wants my attention, he yells, "Rocky" and sounds a lot like his dad!

Over time, the moniker "Mrs. Mommy" grew in meaning to me. Mrs. Mommy is mom, warrior, professional volunteer, special needs advocate, college application counselor and more. I wrestled with, but never regretted, the decision to "retire" and become a stay-at-home mom after Matthew's birth, though at the time I might not have considered it permanent. I am grateful for how hard Brett works to provide that opportunity for our family and me. With each passing year, I embrace the fleeting time with my children and wonder how long I will get to be Mrs. Mommy. Will Matthew stick with this pet name as he matures? Will I feel the draw of a new challenge as my children leave the nest?

The future is unknown, but the lessons I have learned in my role as Mrs. Mommy have had a profound, shaping influence on my life and who I have become. Whether you have just begun this journey, or you are looking for information to support someone in your life, I hope that our family's story is helpful, hopeful, and encouraging to you.

Acknowledgement

"We must find time to stop and thank the people who make a difference in our lives."
  —John F. Kennedy

Without the people acknowledged below and so very many others, I would not be sharing our story with you. I believe now is the time to stop and say thank you!

Brett—you have been my best friend for over thirty years and I cannot imagine life without you. God smiled on me when he chose you for me and I am so blessed to be your wife. Thank you for loving me when life threw us challenges, for listening to all of my crazy ideas and then supporting me every step along the way. This is your story as much as mine.

BethAnne, Peyton and Walker—You guys are the best! I am so proud of each of you, not for your accomplishments, but for your kind and loving hearts. You make my parenting job so much easier. Your unconditional and steadfast love for Matthew makes my heart so happy. I love you all more than you can imagine.

Finally—Matthew. BethAnne, Peyton and Walker may have made me a "mommy", but you made me "Mrs. Mommy." You might have rocked my world just a little bit, but you also brought so much joy (and joyful noise) and love to my life and that of our family. You helped me find my voice and rediscover my love of writing so I could share our story. I love you sweet boy.

My mom deserves special thanks for her unwavering support of my ventures and adventures over the years. Her time with my kids enabled lots of volunteering, relaxing and writing. Her love of Shadow (and his love in return) is unparalleled and so appreciated. I love you, Grand! Miggy and Big Daddy, thank you for all of your love and support. I also want to thank the rest of our family, immediate and extended for their love and support of my writing

Rhonda Robinson—besides being an amazing tutor, you are part of the family. Thank you for loving Matthew as if he were your own. I don't know what we would do without you.

Analyn—you keep us in line and perfectly pressed. Thank you for taking such good care of us.

For our friends who are like family—the ones who listened to my cry over the phone when times were tough, who invited our families into their homes when it wasn't easy, for encouraging me to cut loose and have fun on occasion: Bernstein, Litvak, Robichaux, Robinson and Say Families. Kim Bernstein - thanks for you mad photo editing skills. I appreciate you and couldn't love you more if we were related.

I have so many more people to be thankful for: my teachers, Ms. Edwards, Mrs. Rainwater, Dr. Hall, Dr. Cole, the Drs. Williams and Mr. McBride, that encouraged me to write. They taught me to use my voice and write from the heart to share not what I think people want to hear, but what I believe to be true.

Matthew's teachers and aides over the years all play a part in his journey: from LEP to Capstone to Cordova Park and Sacred Heart Cathedral School Morning Star, you are all indispensable to our family. His physicians and therapists helped us keep our eyes forward and working towards progress even when it seemed like we were sliding backwards. Some of you get Matthew in such a special way and meet him right where he is—Mrs. Zayszly, Ms. Creek, Mrs. Susann, Mrs. Schuck and Mrs. Poller—you are super heroes!

To my fellow special needs' moms, thank you for helping me navigate this trail and sharing your triumphs and challenges with me. I hope this book will help other parents on this journey to see that they are not alone, just as you helped me.

To all my Facebook friends who encouraged me to continue writing and convert my April Awareness posts into a book: You would not be reading this today if not for them. Their words gave me the confidence to pursue my dream of writing of book.

I am thankful to God for putting me on this path. I might not have chosen it, but he knew better than I did. He gave me so much and then gifted me with the grace to handle it. One of my favorite scripture verses is Luke 12:48:

"...to whom much was given, of him much will be required,"

This verse resonates with me because I feel I am so blessed. I do not know how the country girl from Starks, Louisiana, got so lucky. I feel compelled to do much, to give back, to try to pay forward the many gifts shared with me. If just one special needs' parent finds their load a little lighter or feels less alone after reading this book, I will be grateful.

1

The Medical Minefield

The Diagnosis

I think I suffer from PTSD as a result of the pre- and post-autism diagnosis stage of our lives. I recently reviewed Matthew's medical records from the twelve to twenty-four-month age range in my autism writings, and I realized that I never wrote specifically about the diagnosis period. This story would not be complete without a reflection on that time.

Denial exists. And in fact, denial filled every fiber of my being in the months leading up to Matthew's diagnosis. The truth crept in now and again, but denial squashed it every time. I was not alone; nurses, physicians, teachers, family and friends aided and abetted. *There's nothing wrong with Matthew. He's the baby— everyone speaks for him, He's a boy—they are often late to talk.* These statements represent the sentiment and good intentions of those surrounding us. But in the quiet of my heart, I knew Matthew was different. I just did not know why.

I knew we could not begin to help him find his voice until we knew the cause of his challenges. Brett and I began to push for a referral to a psychiatrist, psychologist, neurologist— anyone who could give these symptoms a name, so Matthew could access services and therapy.

Our first referral landed us in the audiology department at Sacred Heart, our local Children's hospital. Maybe Matthew could not hear. I latched on to the false hope that he might be hearing impaired for a minute. I believed this road to recovery would be easier, less bumpy. He passed the hearing screening with flying colors, so we finally got our referrals. Yes, three referrals: a psychiatrist, a neuropsychologist and a neurologist. We quickly scheduled three visits in a condensed time frame.

The first visit, arranged by a pediatrician friend, found us in the office of Dr. S., a local psychiatrist. Dr. S's practice included children and adults, but a concentration of autistic children. He later relocated from Pensacola to practice and research specifically in that field of study. Matthew and I took the day off school on the day of the appointment and I remember being filled with a sense of hope. Strange that I was hopeful, but I knew without a diagnosis, we could not really begin to help or reach Matthew.

After a brief time in the waiting room, Dr. S invited us back into his office. I recall the office being warm and inviting, not at all sterile or cold like a traditional exam room. I also recall Matthew exploring every nook and cranny of the office. Dr. S got on the floor to interact with Matthew as much as possible. This was a first; no other practitioners approached Matthew this way. While they "played," Dr. S asked me questions. Matthew "talked" in his secret language of echolalia and occasionally acknowledged Dr. S.

After about an hour of playing and talking, Dr. S sat down behind his desk and began to explain that Matthew met many of the criteria for the autism spectrum: the echolalia, the lack of eye contact, the lining up of cars and trucks in a very specific order, to name of a few. Dr. S went on to explain that he was optimistic about Matthew's future and his ability to communicate at some level due to the presence of some language, despite how limited it was at that time. I remember feeling oddly relieved. These behaviors had a name: autism. [1]

In the beginning, the new knowledge deflated and overwhelmed me. How would we help Matthew in a community with so few resources? The books I read talked about the extent of services needed and referenced the cities in which they were based. Our city was not on the list. Should we uproot our family to pursue these resources? Our home was here, the children's school was here, Brett's job was here. To pick up and move was not a viable option.

Over the course of the next few months, we saw a pediatric neurologist and a pediatric neuropsychologist. Both confirmed the autism diagnosis. Brett knew more about autism than I did due to his medical background. I vaguely recall trying to explain autism to BethAnne, Peyton and Walker. They wanted answers just like Brett and I did, but unfortunately, I had none. I immersed myself in learning everything I could about autism and its treatments, prognosis, etc. I ordered books and threw half of them away because they were too scientific for me to understand or the suggested treatments were hokey or scary. I watched documentaries about autism. I reached out to people I did not know, but would later come to love, solely because they parented an autistic child.

About that time, a friend who had no idea what we were experiencing invited us to attend the Autism Pensacola Gala at the Hilton Garden Inn on the beach. I remember parts of the night like it was yesterday; other parts seem like a dream and are hazy. But there is one moment neither Brett nor I will ever forget. Shortly after arriving, we ran into a physician friend with an older child on the spectrum. He seemed surprised to see us there and asked how we learned about the event. Brett went on to explain who invited us, and went on to mention that, ironically, Matthew had just received his diagnosis. We, too, had a child on the autism spectrum.

Hearing those words out loud rocked me to the core. I burst into tears and headed straight for the ladies' room, chastising myself along the way for thinking it was a good idea for us to attend this event so soon after receiving Matthew's diagnosis. Our friend then asked Brett a very poignant and thoughtful question that only someone with experience would ask: "How are *you* doing?" He went on to say, "Matthew will be fine, but how are you? This is a tough road and you need to know it's okay to be sad or angry or grieve that the child you have, you will love, he's just not the child you thought you would have." When I returned from the ladies' room moments later, Brett relayed this conversation to me and I was so touched.

Our friend's advice still resonates with me today. I have shared this advice with others numerous times since then—parents in that raw place that we once were in. An autism diagnosis is not a death sentence. Life goes on. Life is different, but it continues. Still, parents need to allow themselves a period to grieve, not a loss of a child, but a loss of an ideal, the plans they had for their child that might no longer be possible.

I took our friend's advice, and I released my anger and my grief and my plans. I cried in the shower and the closet and the car. I gave it all up and started over.

Together with our "team" of therapists, physicians and teachers, we formulated a plan to move forward. We made detours and changes along the way. Even now we are not sure what the finished plan will look like—it is a work in progress.

Eleven years later, I do not experience grief anymore; I experience gratitude, hope and sometimes fear, but not grief. The reality is that I do not know what the future holds for any of my children. I worry about all of them! In reality, I have a little more control over Matthew's future, and I think that scares me most.

"Don't Want A Needle"

One Friday, Matthew and I visited a local laboratory to have blood tests run for two of his physicians. We carefully planned the appointment on a school holiday because of time constraints. We strategically planned his medication schedule for the morning, so he would be most cooperative during the appointment. We arrived at 8:00 am for our 8:30 appointment and as we waited Matthew told me he "didn't want a needle." As soon as we checked in, I reminded the office staff that Matthew is on the autism spectrum and of the extra efforts we made in preparing for the appointment. Around 8:35, the technicians trying to retrieve his labs informed me that we had a little problem. Two of the tests needed to be verbally confirmed with his physician before they could draw them. I reminded them that it was Good Friday and the physician's office was closed. They then suggested we return another day. As politely as I could, but loud enough for the rest of the patients to hear, I again explained our situation, fasting, autism, medication schedule. I even suggested I could call my husband, a physician, and he would be happy to verbally confirm the labs. They reluctantly agreed to draw all of the labs and hold the two in question in cold storage until they could confirm with Matthew's physician on Monday. We proceeded to the phlebotomy chair and Matthew climbed into my lap. He knew the drill from many previous visits. Amazingly, he sat still and watched them draw 14 samples and the same technician I was completely disappointed in moments earlier, regained my trust and admiration for her patience and kindness towards Matthew. I released my anger and thanked the technician for the care she gave Matthew. The expertise she lacked on the administrative side, she more than made up for on the clinical side.

(Written April 20, 2014)

The Quillivant Crisis

Matthew's ADD symptoms compound his autism symptoms, and through the years we've seen the difference the right medication can make on his ability to focus and participate in school, in family outings, and in sports. We have had good experiences and bad experiences, we have titrated to new doses, we have weaned off medications, we have had adverse reactions. I thought we had seen it all until the Quillivant crisis ensued.

For several years, Matthew had taken Quillivant to lessen the challenges ADD presents. It was almost the perfect medication for him: liquid, extended release, easily available. It worked to make his life easier. The only drawbacks were price and the controlled classification of the drug. It was very expensive, but insurance covered the cost after we met our deductible. For those of you who don't know, a controlled drug can only be refilled once every thirty days, has to have a new prescription each month, and requires doctor visits every 90 days or less. Up until that December, we were able to overcome the challenges. Everything was great, until it wasn't.

When BethAnne went to fill his script, the pharmacist at our usual pharmacy explained that he was out of the drug and likely would not have any for a few weeks, nor would any of their other locations in the area. Okay, no problem. I just sent her to another pharmacy chain. Same answer, no availability. My level of concern rose. School was about to start back, and Matthew's ability to function his best in school was strongly impacted by this medication. BethAnne tried one more pharmacy. The pharmacist told us he could get Quillivant by the end of the week. Whew! We had just enough to last until then, and I could ration our remaining supply, just in case.

On Friday, I called the pharmacy to confirm that the medication had arrived before I headed there to pick it up. The pharmacist came to the phone, I asked about the Quillivant and the long pause he took before speaking alarmed me. He went on to explain that the drug was out of stock, on backorder, and he couldn't give me any indication of when it would return to stock. My frustration was high, but Pollyanna here decided if I called enough pharmacies, I would find the medication. After calling every pharmacy in our city and a few in surrounding areas, I faced the realization that a medication change was imminent.

Ugh!

A quick call to the doctor resulted in a trip to Destin—a city an hour and a half from home— to pick up a prescription for a new medication. (His prescribing doctor practices in Destin, and yes, she's worth the drive!) Unfortunately, we learned the new medication had to be ordered and could take several weeks to arrive, so we had to start a new, temporary medication that is readily available to return to school after Christmas. The dread of returning to school (not his favorite place) after a two-week break on a new medication was ominous, and the feeling worsened knowing we would have to make another change within a few weeks. Again, I mustered my inner optimist.

The good news: the transition period was tolerable; temporary medication worked ok; the new medication arrived within one week instead of two, and it seemed work well for a short period. The bad news: the doctor confirmed that the new medication dosage was too low, and our insurance company denied the higher dosage of the new medication. One phone call with the insurance company led me to believe we could resolve the situation, so we paid for the medication out of pocket (ouch), with the hopes of a later reimbursement. Over the course of a few days, I spent hours on the phone with the insurance company and the doctor's office trying to get the higher dosage approved. Ultimately, the insurance company denied the medication because "the published results weren't as good as other similar drugs and they removed it from their formulary". Translation—it's too expensive! So, another quick trip to Destin, another new prescription, another wait for the pharmacy to stock the medication, and another week of highs and lows at school.

I searched Google every so often to see if the back-order status had changed; it had not. I found a Facebook group of ADD parents that contained pages of comments with stories like Matthew's: parents explaining that their children were taking this liquid form because they could not swallow pills parents discussing the fact that the shortage had come out of nowhere and the release date was constantly being extended— on and on. The good news was that over the course of about six weeks, we finally settled on a medication that appeared to be effective for Matthew (even though it was a non-chewable pill that he chooses to chew instead of swallow), insurance company will cover it and pharmacy can keep in stock. The bad news—I don't believe this medication is quite as effective as Quillivant, but Quillivant is still back-ordered.

Medicinal Benefits

One Saturday morning in the fall when I was trying to sleep in, I heard Matthew come stomping down the hall saying, "But I don't want to tell Mom!" with Brett following close behind insisting, "Go tell your mom what you did." I immediately popped up in the bed wondering just what had prompted this exchange. What was broken or opened? I could only imagine.

Matthew walked in the bedroom saying, "I'm sorry, Mom, but I don't like medicine." I insisted, "Matthew, we have to take our medicine. It's not a choice!"

Brett gave me a "you're never going to believe this look" and then turned to Matthew and told him to take me to the office.

We walked down the hall, through the kitchen, to the office, with Matthew repeating, "But I don't like medicine," over and over again. Once in the office, Brett suggested that Matthew show me what was in the desk drawer. Imagine my surprise when Matthew opened the drawer below the computer to a pile of morning medicine. When I say pile, I mean 30-40 pills. I was aghast. No words, well actually lots of words were running through my mind, most of them words I rarely say aloud. I wanted to laugh because if I didn't laugh, I might cry. I found my mean mom voice and lectured Matthew about the necessity of taking his medicine, how it helps him, the positive benefits. Again, he stated, "I don't like medicine and it tastes bad!"

I explained that no medicine equals no screens—something he wants and definitely understands as a consequence for poor behavior.

We excused him from the office, and I took an immediate inventory of the pills at least 30 days of morning attention meds and mood stabilizer. Now, that might explain the behavior problems Matthew had experienced recently at school. He had exhibited impulsivity and lack of focus for the past month or so. I thought he needed a medication adjustment and had scheduled an appointment for the next week.

Perhaps he didn't need an adjustment—maybe he just needed to take his prescribed medication! I beat myself up for letting this occur, for not checking to see if he swallowed his meds, for not asking the right questions, for everything I could think of that had led to this Mom Fail.

More details emerged. When I would bring the medication to him in the office each morning, he would wait until I left the room to spit the pills into the drawer. Let that last sentence sit with you for a minute. Bummer, right? I should have been angry that he was being so deceptive. However, a part of me was thrilled because it showed a higher level of executive functioning than I gave him credit for. So, it was a good news bad news sort of thing: bad news that we experienced weeks of poor choices at school that were completely avoidable; good news that his level of thinking and planning was higher than we thought.

I 'fessed up to his teachers via email and explained that we might have an explanation for his recent behavioral regressions. On that following Tuesday, I explained the weekend's turn of event to the doctor. She gave Matthew a quick lecture on the necessity of his medications and how they positively enhance his life. She explained to me that it could take up to three weeks for one of them to get back to full effectiveness. Ugh. She then suggested that we might want to look around the house for other hiding places—who knew how long this had been going on?

Fortunately, the doctor's takeaway was similar to mine. While we don't encourage dishonesty or deception, on this occasion, it revealed some skills we did not know were there. We just had to figure out how to positively channel those skills—AND make sure he swallowed his pills before we walk away.

Almost immediately, Matthew's problem behaviors improved. At least for this round of medications, we have some assurance that they make a difference for Matthew.

(Written April 1, 2019)

[1] At that time, we still had the diagnosis of Asperger's and Autism. Today both fall under the Autism Spectrum Disorder (ASD) diagnosis code.

2

Family Ties

Going to College

With a senior in high school in the house, we spend a lot of time talking about college. I was not sure how much Matthew was taking in or how much he understood. However, on Friday when we were walking away from his school, he confirmed to me just how aware he is and how much he hears. He said, "Steve is going to college." For those of you unfamiliar with Blue's Clues, the original lead character was replaced when he went to college. Then he said, "Andy is going to college." Andy in Toy Story 3 gives the toys away when he goes to college. Finally, he said, "NaNa (BethAnne) is going to college." I said, "Yes, Matthew she is…" and a big lump filled my throat. He knows and communicates his emotions through his favorite shows…but he knows.

(Written April 26, 2015)

Unconditional Love

About twelve years ago when Brett and I told BethAnne, Peyton and Walker that we had a surprise for them, BethAnne quickly exclaimed, "We're getting a puppy!" Her face fell for a second (or two), when Brett said, "No, Mom's having a baby!" She, Peyton and Walker quickly mustered some excitement for the news.

Upon his birth, Matthew was surrounded with love: two big sisters who remembered everything Matthew needed that their tired mama forgot, and a big brother who just couldn't wait to teach Matthew everything he knew. For almost two years, we just coasted along. Happy party of six. Then Matthew began to plateau, possibly even regress. No speech, very little eye contact, lining up toys by size, by color, and so on. Brett and I began our research and went to many doctors' appointments. The older kids asked tough questions. Unfortunately, we didn't have any immediate or easy answers.

As test results came in, the diagnosis became clear: PDD-NOS, pervasive developmental disorder-not otherwise specified, in other words - Autism. As an accountant, I knew nothing about the disorder and certainly didn't have the tools or words to make it clear to a 10, 9 and 6-year old. We did our best to explain it and the uncertainty of how and to what extent Matthew would progress. Amazingly, once they learned it wasn't terminal (and thank God it is not), BethAnne, Peyton and Walker made it a point to learn about autism and overnight became advocates for Matthew.

While none of them would admit it, it hasn't always been easy to have a little brother on the autism spectrum. There were communication barriers, there was frustration, there was disappointment. He has, at times, wreaked havoc on their worlds. For Walker, it came in the form of broken trophies. One evening several years ago, Matthew was very quiet, and when Walker went into the room to check on him, he found all of his trophies in pieces on the floor. He asked Matthew "Why?" and Matthew explained that he was the soccer monster from Backyardigans.

Brett and I were both heartbroken, but Walker simply said, "It's not the actual trophies that matter, it's the work that went into them."

Another time, we were having some kids over as Peyton was leaving for camp in the next few days. Once again, Matthew was quiet. I searched for him and finally found him in the laundry room. He had been busy. He had emptied all of Peyton's items packed for camp, along with storage boxes, laundry baskets, all of our containers of nails, tape, zip ties and so on. He then used the boxes to build a "ladder" to get to something that caught his attention. It took us hours to repack and reorganize, but Peyton never complained.

Of course, Matthew didn't leave BethAnne out. She had purchased a beautiful, working, antique typewriter and had it on her desk. One day, she returned to her room and Matthew was "typing." His typing was rather destructive and broke several of the keys. While she was disappointed, she moved on with little anger at him and recognized his curiosity and love for letters.

All of the havoc is erased with love. My older children show Matthew unconditional love, boundless respect, and acceptance every day. They are advocates, not just for Matthew but others who are different in their schools, on their teams, and in the public at large. From young ages, they became very independent, because they didn't want to add to our stress. They argued less and stopped saying, "That's not fair," because they saw that life is not always fair. They still work hard at everything they do, because they see their little brother work so hard to master things that come easily to others. They accept that one day, when Brett and I are gone or no longer able, they may assume responsibility for Matthew. While we hope, plan and work towards independence every day, we are also realists. We have a Plan B. They all willingly and gladly accept their roles in Plan B.

I asked each of them what was the best and hardest part of having an autistic sibling and asked if I could share that with you. BethAnne worries about how other people treat him and not always being there to put an end to it. The best part for her is trying to change how others treat him when she can, and that in spending time with him, she gets to experience his great moments that many others do not. Peyton says the most challenging time occurs when Matthew is struggling and there is nothing she can do except encourage him. She says he has positively changed her perspective on life and made her a much more accepting person. Finally, Walker says the hardest part is when his friends do not understand autism and he must explain it to them. The best is playing with Matthew. When they play, Matthew is "happier than any kid in the world" and he shows his appreciation through his smile (and he doesn't always smile).

I recently asked Matthew what he his favorite thing to do was with each of his siblings. He likes to go to Disney World with and get mail from Na-Na

(BethAnne), and he likes to go to Utah skiing with Peyton. He likes to play outside with Walker and ride on the scooter and play hide and seek. He said, "They are my friends." They were his first friends, and they are his best friends and his best advocates.

I share this part of our story today, not for any pity or praise. I share it because I want you to see the positive impact that Matthew and his siblings have on each other every day. I want to thank BethAnne Parra, Peyton Parra and Walker Parra for constantly reminding me what unconditional love looks like. They show it in their love for Matthew every day.

(Written April 7, 2016)

Dad Can Fix Anything

Unbridled curiosity, focused attention to detail and communication challenges (that can drive him to frustration) accompany Matthew's autism. During the years, these attributes yielded a variety of opportunities for Brett to use his handyman skills. He repaired sheetrock because Matthew pulled the curtain rod hardware out of the wall. When asked why, Matthew explained he was "swinging like Tarzan." We responded that we do not swing in the house from anything, curtains, ceiling fans, door frames, or anything else.

Matthew takes things literally, so we learned—sometimes the hard way—that we needed to be very specific in our instructions of what to do, and, more importantly, what NOT to do.

Let's just say that Brett's puzzle solving skills evolved a lot over the last nine years. He pieced and then glued back together countless glassware, trophies, even a wooden chair. Now, Matthew was not the only one who provided these opportunities— BethAnne, Peyton and Walker contributed to this professional development as well. Brett has put books back together, taping pages very meticulously. He learned the best way to get crayons, ink and permanent marker off the walls from budding artists. He even figured out how to get chocolate syrup out of white carpet. I married a man with

13

hidden talents.

Of course, he also uses his medical skills. Anytime anyone in the house has an injury or ailment, they ask for dad, "because he's a doctor"–or, as Matthew stated, "because dad's a doctor, and he can fix anything." He stitched up Walker's head, removed countless splinters, cared for broken bones, cleaned up bodily fluids—you name it. Thank goodness, because I get a little squeamish! I know he does much more complicated medical things at work, but we are really grateful for the ones he does at home.

Recently, Brett put his surgical skills to work at home. Matthew had been very quiet for a while, a little unusual for him, when suddenly he walked in and asked for Brett. I could see that he had a toy in his hand, but he was kind of hiding it from me. I sensed that he didn't want to show me what it was. He asked when dad would be home. He needed him to fix something.

I convinced Matthew to show me what he was holding. He slowly lifted up beloved Woody with his left arm dangling by a thread. I didn't really need a further explanation, but in his best Andy voice he said, "Oh I forgot, I don't want to play with you anymore. You're broken." Luckily, Brett walked in from work, and Matthew immediately shifted his attention to Dad. He showed him Woody's broken arm and asked him to fix it—"because you're a doctor". Out came the sewing kit, and after selecting the right needle for doll arms, Dr. Daddy went right to work. Not sure how many stitches this patient required, but Woody was made whole, and Matthew was thrilled.

(Written April 9, 2017)

He's Not Heavy, He's My Brother

BethAnne, Peyton and Walker love Matthew to infinity and beyond! Over the years, they've taken on whatever role necessary to help him succeed: playmate, teacher, therapist, babysitter.

The early years were hard. They all had to make sacrifices, whether they realized it or not. Walker celebrated when he found out he was going to have a little brother. He planned to teach him how to play sports, to make mischief, to harass the big sisters. When he realized that Matthew might not learn to do those things because of his autism and epilepsy, I know he experienced a temporary sense of loss or disappointment, but he never spoke of it.

All three of the "big" kids assumed greater responsibilities for Matthew as they and he grew older. To a certain extent, they created a niche for themselves. BethAnne was the mother hen, making sure he took his medication and got to bed on time. She also introduced him to all things Disney. Peyton, thankfully, helped fulfill his camping desires, pitching a tent in the backyard and convincing Brett they should take Matthew camping. Walker was his first and best playmate. They made up a game called "press your button" years ago and they still play it together today.

They all celebrate Matthew and his achievements, big and small. They proudly introduce him to their friends and classmates and encourage their peers to reach out and get to know their little brother. They learned to be advocates for Matthew and others like him.

BethAnne, Peyton, and Walker wrote and presented speeches about their brother while in elementary and middle school. They participate in service projects benefitting autism and epilepsy. They don't just teach awareness, they model acceptance. Not just acceptance of Matthew, but of anyone who reminds them of Matthew.

Over the past two years, as BethAnne and Peyton moved away to college, Walker's role as caretaker grew. Walker matured as he assumed these additional responsibilities. This maturity increased his awareness of other autistic and special needs individuals, and he began to advocate for them. People can be cruel and say things that hurt, especially when they don't know you have a brother with autism. Walker does not sit back and take this talk lightly; he takes the opportunity to teach and defend.

Matthew idolizes Walker these days. He began swim lessons in the fall and wants to "swim fast" like Walker. He refers to Walker as his best friend. He's sad when Walker is away, and I can see we will face a big adjustment when Walker goes to college like BethAnne, Peyton, and "Andy." They have a mutual admiration society, these two! I love what they learn from each other, what I have learned from them, and what I hope others learn from them.

When I reflect on the special relationships Matthew share with his siblings, I think of this verse of lyrics from the song, *He Ain't Heavy, He's My Brother* (by The Hollies), I believe the words illustrate their love for Matthew:

His welfare is of my concern
   No burden is he to bear
   We'll get there
   For I know
   He would not encumber me
   He ain't heavy, he's my brother
   If I'm laden at all
   I'm laden with sadness
   That everyone's heart
   Isn't filled with the gladness
   Of love for one another [2]

(Written April 15, 2017)

Sweet Dreams

"Mrs. Mommy, what do you dream about?"

"What?"

"Mrs. Mommy, what do you dream about?"

After I recovered from my surprise at his question, I responded with a typical mom answer; another question. "What do you dream about Matthew?"

"I dream about my iPad, McDonald's, staying home all day, sticking with Buzz Lightyear, going on trips for 100 sleeps. Mom, what do you dream about?"

"I dream about writing a book." *Wait, what? Did I just say that out loud? I don't know how to write a book. Don't know the first step to take. I better say something else.*

"Matthew, I also dream about sleep and having all my family in the nest at the same time."

"Mrs. Mommy, what does Dad dream about?"

"LSU winning a national championship! Family vacations that everyone can go on. Camping. Healthcare before the EHR."

"What about Walker?"

"Swimming in college! Summer! Having enough food to fill him up when he's hungry!"

"Peyton?"

"Camp Mac. Sunrises. Getting into medical school."

"BethAnne?" (He actually said BethAnne and not his usual NaNa)

"Sleep (she's an architecture student). Getting her dream job. Traveling the globe in style."

"Grand?"

"Spending time with all of her treasures, Texas and Florida."

"Miggy and Big Daddy?"

"Miggy dreams about dancing and having all of her people together and Big Daddy dreams about his next nap and all of his adventures!"

I turned the table on him at this point, I asked "What does Mrs. Susann dream about?"

"School." (She's his teacher)

"Mrs. Robinson?" (His after school tutor and family friend)

"Going to the movies."

"Caroline?"

"Saying 'come here sweet son'" (This is his friend who helps him at school; he repeats this phrase like I imagine he hears it from her. It's awesome.)

"Zoe?" (one of his classmates)

"Having friends and doing fun things together."

About this point he said, "I'm done with dreaming." I finally took a breath and realized this is one of the longest, back and forth, real conversations we've ever had. We really talked, not in movie talk, not about a movie or episode or character, but about REAL PEOPLE AND THEIR DREAMS! This, people, is the kind of thing that autism moms and dads dream about. I wish

I knew what prompted and sustained it for so long.

"Hey, Matthew, can I add one more thing to my list? I dream about having more conversations like this with you!"

A Sibling is the Lens Through Which You See Your Childhood

I follow quite a few blogger moms on social media. Some are special needs moms, Catholic moms, moms to many, moms to one, moms to children of all ages. They all have something to share, something I can learn from. Recently on one of those pages, a follower asked a mom of three, one of whom happens to have Down syndrome, if she felt she was "short-changing" her other children, or if they were jealous of her writing about that child or the amount of time her child with Down syndrome required. She answered openly and honestly. The question has haunted me quite a bit since then.

If the title above is true, I hope the lens through which BethAnne, Peyton and Walker see their childhood is a clear one. Do they feel jealous or short-changed by having Matthew in their world? I hope not. I hope they see all the joy Matthew brings to our family. You could ask them, and I know they would say they are richer for having him in their world. I bet they would all say he's "my favorite sibling!"

He entered their world (and ours) as a bit of surprise. And for all of us, the surprises have kept coming, sometimes requiring sacrifices. Special Needs or not, all siblings learn to sacrifice for each other throughout their childhood and into their adult life. School conflicts, sport conflicts, missed birthdays, and hand-me-downs just a tip of the iceberg.

The years leading to Matthew's diagnosis were a whirlwind. BethAnne, Peyton and Walker just rolled with it. As we received answers and prognosis, they continued to roll with it. They were not simply siblings; they were helpers, care-givers, playmates and defenders. Their maturity and selfless-ness amazed me then and continues to amaze me now. They learned about autism, they became advocates, they loved Matthew unconditionally. I like to think autism brought them closer together and gave them even more of a shared bond than the traditional sibling bond.

Loving Matthew did more than increase their bonds as siblings; knowing and loving Matthew made them better people. Of course, I'm prejudiced, but I believe living with Matthew helped them become more compassionate, empathetic people. They learned to work hard, they watched him work so hard to do things that came so easily to them. They watched how tired we were caring for him and they tried to be less work, to carry a heavier load at home, to make good choices. They are compassionate to others, they are accepting of those who are different, and they have a great capacity to love and serve others. They each, in their own way, want to leave the world a better place. I'm proud of them and grateful to them. I hope Matthew knows how blessed he is to have them.

I would tell my other autism mom friends, with younger children, that your other children will be okay. In fact, they will likely be better than okay. Be honest with them, even at a young age. Buy them books about autism and read those books with them. Involve them in the care of your child with autism, whether they are younger or older. Teach them about their sibling's challenges and make sure they uncover their own gifts as well. Talk to them about autism—do not be afraid to use the words. Make them part of the team. Let them know you love them and that their sibling does, too, even when he does not know how to show it or say it.

(Written April 30, 2018)

An Inside View

Having Matthew as a brother has shaped each of our children in different ways. We were discussing life with Matthew recently, and each wanted to share some reflections on life in our house. So, let me share their thoughts, in their own words.

Walker, Brett, Matthew, Mrs. Mommy, BethAnne and Peyton (photo credit: Ashley Uptain, edited by Kim Bernstein)

Walker

Growing up with Matthew as a little brother made a huge impact on who I am today. He made me appreciate all the little victories in life. There are times when I think to myself that I'm not fast enough, smart enough or good enough, but then I reflect back to times when Matthew had to work really hard to learn something we take for granted, like when he learned to talk. Most people think of speaking as just something you learn to do in life, like it is instinctive, but it was a major accomplishment for Matthew.

At around four years old and after two years of extensive speech therapy,

Matthew finally started using words and phrases we could understand. How hard he worked to communicate verbally and continues to work to learn new things makes me approach challenges from a more positive perspective. It reminds me to be grateful for the talents I possess no matter how small because there are others who would be happy to be right where I am.

Life with him is not always perfect, but not for the reasons you might think. The autism stuff I've grown accustomed to, and it's just part of Matthew and life with Matthew. It's the normal little brother stuff that I never expected from him that throws me off guard. Sometimes when I walk into the room he is in, he immediately tells me to GET OUT. He always wants to use my stuff, and when I have friends over, he wants their attention, but that's not autism— that's just what little brothers do. I know that when I am away at school, I'm going to miss this guy and his shenanigans more than he will ever know!

Peyton

I've always been grateful for Matthew. I love his contagious belly laugh, his love for camping and his childlike innocence. I love his honesty—you know what you're getting when you talk to Matthew. He tells you like it is, whether you're ready to hear it or not. For example, I will ask him if he wants to go play outside or listen to a certain song... and I know, without a doubt, that he is going to tell me just what he wants. I wish we could all be a little bit more honest with each other like this. But you get the point, I am a big fan of his honesty.

Another thing I have ALWAYS loved about Matthew is his memory. This kid remembers the most minuscule details and recalls them years after the fact - it's remarkable. I love my little brother, Matthew!

One thing I didn't always love, though, was Autism. I don't have the biggest collection of childhood memories, but I can never forget the feeling in the house after Mom and Dad sat us down for the first time, telling us about Matthew and his autism. I honestly can't find the right word for how I felt - it wasn't sad, it was not curious, it wasn't frustrated, it wasn't shocked, it wasn't confused, but perhaps a mix of all of those with a little bit of hope added in.

I immediately questioned everything, not so much out loud, but at least in my head. I asked, what is Autism? Why does Matthew have it? What caused this? What does this look like long term for Matthew? What about for our family? Will he ever be able to talk to us? Does he know he has Autism? You get the point - lots and lots of questions. I was upset for Matthew, for my parents. While I loved him all the same, I was honestly quite frustrated with the whole situation and couldn't see the light in all of this. I saw the obstacles. I imagined how tough Matthew's journey would be, how expensive the medicine and doctor's visits would be, and more than anything, I imagined how much this would weigh on my parents. After questioning and questioning, I was even frustrated with God. It didn't seem to make sense. Then, slowly, my heart softened little by little and I began to see Matthew, his autism and the entire story in a new light.

In very small ways, the Lord began to reveal to me the beauty in Autism. Yes - the beauty in Autism. Years later, I realize that autism spectrum disorder is quite a beautiful thing. Autism has been a source of unity within the Parra family - together, we see and experience the funny moments, the awkward ones, the frustrating, the inspiring, and everything in between. Also, having a sibling with Autism has made me interact with others in a new way. Now, when I walk into a room, instead of asking myself, "Who looks the most fun to talk to?" I ask myself, "Who seems nervous or alone? Who's being left out?" I find so much joy in meeting those who are different than me, and I say "different" not just referring to Autism. I strive to see Christ in each person I encounter, regardless of our similarities or differences. I certainly fail to do this sometimes, but continually remind myself of this daily.

As I grew to see Autism in a new light, I discovered a deeper peace in Autism. God created Matthew just as he is - Autism and all - and he couldn't have done a better job. Autism is part of what makes Matthew "Matthew," the little brother I love and adore so much! So, after all these years, the questions certainly haven't stopped. They've grown in number but also have changed in nature. Instead of questioning God about the situation, I ask how I can use this for the good of others. I ask myself, "What have I learned from Matthew?" I wonder, "How can I be a better sibling to Matthew?" "How can

I better serve others who may be different than me?" "How can I empower others through this?"

Nowadays, I thank God. I thank Him for giving me and my family the strength and patience to get through the long days. Parra fam, y'all know what I mean!! I thank Him for all the joyful moments, like when we realized that Matthew, at a very young age, could seamlessly sing the alphabet backwards. I thank Him for bringing us tighter through this crazy journey. I praise Him for Matthew, Walker, Bethie, for my humble, selfless mother, my incredibly strong father. And sometimes, I even thank Him for Autism.

BethAnne

I have a handful of nicknames bestowed to me by my siblings – Bethie, Batman, and Nana. The last of which was given by Matthew, before he could pronounce my name; though, recently, he has come to correct any of us who call me by his moniker, saying, "No, it's BethAnne." Who would have thought that I'd have hated the sound of my name so much, now the sound of Matthew growing up?

There's so much change in our lives, and in him, exacerbated by the fact that I am away at school, a reality that Matthew adjusted to more quickly than I can admit to. Every time I return home, it's unavoidable – he is taller, obsessed with some new show, and telling new jokes. Our relationship has changed, too, and he plays on my guilt with an expert hand. When I am home, we bake cakes and watch movies and switch beds (a full for a bunkbed, not exactly an even trade). I can't say no to him, and he knows it.

As the oldest, I hate to watch my younger siblings grow up but they're doing it so wonderfully, becoming more driven and independent and I therefore must concede. So, yes, there's a part of me that's sad each time he insists on calling me BethAnne, but the other part that can't wait to see the person he is becoming. There's not a lot to do to stop it anyways.

Matthew

—I thought it would be interesting to see what he had to say about his siblings as well:

My favorite thing about Walker is playing the skateboard video game with him in his room.

My favorite thing about Peyton is the hugs she gives me.

My favorite thing about BethAnne is that she brings me surprises when she comes home from college.

(Written April 29, 2019)

[2] The Hollies. Russel, Bob. Scott, Bobby. "He Ain't Heavy, He's My Brother." *The Best of the Hollies, Epic, 1973, Track 7.* www.metrolyrics.com/he-aint-heavy-hes-my-brother-lyrics-hollies.

3

"Matthew Ristom Parra – The Movie"

"How Many Sleeps?"

Matthew's development, and the development of many autistic individuals, progresses at a different pace. Some things ahead of schedule while other things behind the "typical" schedule. From an early age, his memory astounded us. He remembered minute details about places we visited or where things were hidden. However, his concept of time and ability to measure the passage of time were fuzzier. He knew the days of the weeks and months of the year, and the concepts of forward and backward, but he couldn't apply them his life.

For years, when he asked to do something, and I told him when we would do it later or on Thursday, he would simply reply "tomorrow." Everything was "tomorrow," even if it might actually be days, weeks or months away. I struggled with how to help him understand. We marked out days on calendars, but it still did not sink in.

One day I overheard Grand, my mom, talking on the phone to her granddaughter in Texas and they discussed mom's upcoming visit to Texas. They talked about what they would do and where they would go. Near the end, I heard my mom say she would be there in 5 sleeps. Afterwards, I asked my mom about it and she explained before every trip they counted down the sleeps until she arrived. We moved on to another topic and temporarily "sleeps" were out of my mind.

Not long after that conversation, Matthew and I were talking about an upcoming trip of our own. He gets very excited about travel and wanted to know if we were leaving "tomorrow". I told him we were leaving on Thursday, in 5 sleeps. He thought for a moment and then said, "5 sleeps, then 4 sleeps, then 3 sleeps, then 2 sleeps, then 1 sleep, then zero sleeps." So, there we were with a new way to measure time. Counting sleeps stuck and we now use that term to measure how many "sleeps" until the weekend, until we go to Grand's house, until school is out, until the next trip. It is comforting and routine to him. He thrives on routine.

"How many sleeps?" is just one more example of how finding the right way to present a topic makes all the difference, not just to autistic children, but to anyone who might not learn or comprehend things the traditional way[KT1]
.

The Magic of Butterflies
"There is nothing in a caterpillar that tells you it's going to be a butterfly."
- Richard Buckminster Fuller

Matthew's love of butterflies began with an episode of Jay Jay the Jet Plane featuring Breezy the Butterfly. Matthew watched this episode hundreds of times when he was younger and occasionally still searches for it on YouTube. A few years later, Disney's Little Einsteins helped "butterfly" find his family's migration party and along the way learned about the life cycle and migration patterns of the Monarch Butterfly.

That introduction was all Matthew needed. Since then, he has gravitated to books, movies, TV shows, and toys that showcase butterflies. He recently used his knowledge of butterflies to complete a science project on animal adaptations. When we sat down to research and dictate his project, he surprised me with his appropriate use of words like "metamorphosis" and "migration." He easily explained the life cycle of the butterfly and the importance of the chrysalis. He told me how some of the colors found on the Monarch caterpillar and Monarch butterfly were the same and some were different. His eyes lit up when he spoke of them.

Once, at the end of the school day, Matthew's teacher reminded him to tell me what he discovered at school that day. He excitedly told me, a "Monarch caterpillar!" As it turns out, Matthew found the caterpillar on a leaf in their class garden. and they put the caterpillar in the butterfly habitat in the room to see what would happen next. Actually, there were two caterpillars! The class watched each caterpillar form its chrysalis the next day. Every day after school, Matthew updated me on the progress. Finally, after several days, Matthew excitedly told me about watching the butterflies emerge from the chrysalis. He named them Matthew and Breezy==imagine that! The class released them from the habitat and Matthew renewed his search for "another caterpillar."

When I stop and think about the parallel between our life cycle and that of the butterfly, I am awestruck. We all experience our time as a caterpillar, retreat into our chrysalis, and emerge later with our wings. I am also astounded by Matthew and the lessons he teaches me every day. I just have to stop and listen.

The Age of Innocence

If you venture into Matthew's room, you learn what he loves: all things Disney Pixar, the Wiggles, Nick, Jr., PBS kids, his beloved iPad, and McDonald's. If you don't know him and you had to guess his age based on his room, your answer might be younger than his actual age of 11 and a half years old. Furthermore, you might assume that either a) his mom needs to update his room to match his age, b) his interests are really different than most kids his own age or c) both. B is correct—his interests are really different than most kids his age, and that's ok!

Matthew has loved the Wiggles from the moment he first saw them: the music, the humor, the use of color. We found some Wiggle figures from Australia on eBay so that Matthew could act out his favorite episodes. Disney Pixar posters from his favorite movies adorn his walls, figures fill his toy bins, and books line his shelves. Look further and you will discover that characters from Blue's Clues and Higglytown Heroes hide away in drawers and suitcases. New toys come and go with new movies and TV shows. Old favorites move up and down on the popularity chart over time, but typically stay in the family.

At one point, before I made my peace with autism, I tried to introduce more age-appropriate toys and movies. I decided Matthew needed to watch Sponge Bob. Other kids his age watched Sponge Bob. It might give him something in common with neuro-typical kids his age, right? Well, Matthew was not interested in Sponge Bob, and my older kids threw a fit. "You never let us watch Sponge Bob why do you let Matthew? Do you know what he says or how he talks? Matthew is going to repeat that stuff and you will be horrified!!" You know what? They were right, and Sponge Bob left the island.

This episode prompted me to do a little research and to look at studies on age appropriateness and autism. I learned that some people with autism retain interest in things they loved as a child, and many adults with autism encourage allowing autistic children to retain those interests. In fact, those items provide comfort and joy that help autistics to cope with and get through challenging times. Matthew worked hard all the time: trying to keep up in school, attending speech, occupational and ABA therapy, applying what he learns in those therapies, etc. I realized that he needed to enjoy his down time and refuel for the next challenge.

Anyone who does not live in a cave knows that adult coloring books are all the rage right now. From Barnes and Noble to Target to Anthropologie, many retail outlets promote adult coloring books of all kinds: nature, architecture, Harry Potter. Experts explain the "therapeutic" benefits of coloring, so it's okay for adults to walk around with coloring books and crayons—but not necessarily a Big Red Car or Buzz Lightyear. Well, if it is ok for all ages to color, it is equally ok for them to play with toys. Right?

With the advice of adult autistics in mind and the actual evidence of the joy Matthew finds in his favorites, I no longer feel the need to push age-appropriate toys. We work on, and will continue to work on, age-appropriate language and behavior. We must progress. But down time is down time, and play time must be fun, so Murray, Anthony, Jeff and Greg will stay. (Yes, those are the original Wiggles, Matthew is a purist.) If you see us at Target singing your favorite Wiggles song, like *Hats* or *Fruit Salad*, join us and feel the joy of childhood again.

The "Tired" Wiggles

The Wiggles have been present in my life in some way, shape or form for the last 20 years. Read that again, 20 years. That's a long time!

Some of you might not be as familiar with their history as the Parras, so let me give you a quick primer. The Wiggles began in 1991 in Sydney, Australia. They originally had five members: Greg, Murray, Jeff, Philip and Anthony, but we don't really count Philip who was only around for one album. The "real" Wiggles are Greg, Murray, Jeff and Anthony. Jeff and Anthony got their start in music in a rock band called The Cockroaches, when they disbanded Anthony went back to school and pursued a degree in early childhood education. His growing knowledge of education combined with his musical interests ultimately led to the creation of The Wiggles.

Their first album was almost a research project with each song having a specific educational value. After a couple of years, they quit their day jobs and pursued the early childhood music market full-time. After strong success in Australia, they entered the American market in the early 2000s and rose to *stardom*. They introduced new characters like Wags the Dog, Dorothy the Dinosaur and Captain Feathersword. Due to age and health issues, some of the original cast retired and the group now consists of Anthony, Lachlan, Simon and Emma. Matthew is a purist and prefers the originals!

The older kids watched and listened to The Wiggles because I thought they were wholesome and somewhat educational. Eventually, they moved on to other things, and I thought we might be done. However, when Matthew came along, The Wiggles became a permanent fixture. I think the original attraction was the music, but also there was something about the color-coded shirts, Greg (red), Murray (yellow), Jeff (purple) and Anthony (blue). Matthew associated stores with their primary brand color, characters, etc. Target is the red store, Publix is the green store and Wal-Mart is the blue store, so The

Wiggles fit right into his color-coded world.

Before he spoke clearly, Matthew would sing along with The Wiggles, from **Hot Potato** and **Fruit Salad** in the early days to **Toot, Toot, Chuga, Chuga Big Red Car** and **Rockabye Your Bear.** Matthew owns copies of most of their videos on either DVD or VHS or both. I tried purchasing him one of the new videos; he watched about 2 songs and asked, "Where are the other friends?"

I thought about how to explain where they were in a way he would understand. I told him that some the *old* Wiggles retired because it was time to let some new singers have a turn. He didn't know what retired meant so I said it was someone who doesn't work in a job anymore.

He said, "Like you!"

"Yes, Matthew, like me."

He went on, "Are you tired? Is that why you retired?"

"No, Matthew, it does not always mean you are tired. I retired to take care of you, BethAnne, Peyton and Walker. Does that make sense?"

My efforts were in vain.

He continued, "The old Wiggles are tired, so we have new ones."

I gave up.

The Wiggles are ever-present in his mind and therefore our world. I don't think a day passes that he doesn't sing a song from The Wiggles. My favorite is **Georgia's Song**, a lullaby Anthony wrote for his daughter. Matthew sometimes sings it to me during our nighttime routine and his sweet voice singing warms my heart. I want to share the lyrics with you; I hope you enjoy:

Hear the wind in the trees
See the leaves falling down
Feel the soft rain on your face
As we walk around
Smell the flower's sweet scent
Taste the food that I bring
Daddy's right here with you now
And it's your song that I sing [3]

The next time you hear or see The Wiggles, I hope you will think of Matthew and smile.

Do You Remember the Time...?

I feel with each passing year, my memory declines a little bit more. I remember fewer and fewer of the details of my childhood. I do not really forget a face, but names are beginning to escape me. The major events of the children's lives remain etched in my mind, but some of the day-to-day activities fade a bit with each passing day. I guess that is just part of growing up (or old).

Ironically, Matthew's memory is incredible. Let me rephrase that- Matthew's memory of events and places amazes me. He cannot always recall the things he needs to remember for school. His processing challenges seem to muddy his recall of academic-type material. It is unfortunate that his talent for remembering is not an equal opportunity sort of thing.

About 8 years ago, I started the tradition of gifting each of the children with a photo album that captures the events of the previous calendar. I personalize each one to capture the highlights that child for that year and include shared family photos. During the awkward years, the older kids did not always love their books, but as they grow older, they appreciate the effort and love that goes into each page. Matthew, on the other hand, LOVES the books. Inadvertently, they became a tool to work on his memory skills. One of his Matthewisms, "Do you remember the time...?" originated one day when we reviewed his books. The books are also a memory tool for me. As we look at the books, I can remember the time or the vacation or the Halloween costume.

Now the phrase "do you remember the time" pops up during our time in the car. We might be on a road trip or driving to and from swim practice or on the way home from school.

One day, Grand and I visited during the drive to Louisiana, while Matthew quietly played on his iPad in the back seat. Suddenly, he asked, "Do you remember the time I got lost in the attic of the cabinet? I couldn't find my way out. I was trying to escape."

I immediately remembered the time and laughed out loud. Brett and I went to Jackson's for an anniversary meal. We left the four kids at home. Matthew could not have been more than four years old. A family friend's daughter drove us to dinner and made plans to pick us up, so we could drink some celebratory wine and not worry about the drive home. We had a lovely meal and did not hear a word from the kids. When our driver returned, we were barely buckled in when she said, "Everything is ok, but… we got a call from the kids earlier because they couldn't find Matthew." (What? They couldn't find Matthew?) She continued, "Mom and Dad went down to your house and learned Matthew wasn't lost. He was just stuck in a cabinet in your game room. Well not actually in the cabinet, more in the wall. They could hear his voice; they just couldn't see him. My dad figured out where he was and they were able to talk him through climbing out. Everything's fine now."

Obviously, we couldn't wait to get home and see this for ourselves. As it turns out, one of our cabinets was under a built-in bookshelf with a false front. Matthew climbed into the cabinet to "hide" and discovered the opening to the wall behind the false front and tried to climb through. He was "escaping through the hatch".

Matthew went on to ask me if I remembered the time, he hurt his finger on "the coffee thing at a house by a barn." At first, I had no idea what he was talking about. Then I remember a house we rented in Maine several years ago had a barn-like structure behind it.

I asked if it was the house with a bird inside. He said, "Yes, I hurt my finger on the coffee thing in the house with the bird."

I am not sure I even knew he hurt his finger on that trip. He spoke so clearly about events that occurred so long ago like they were yesterday, but he struggles to tell me what he ate for lunch. That is how this game works for us. He remembers a time or event that I did not realize made such an impression on him or that I do not recall, and I remember how he "is wonderfully made" (Psalm 139:14).

A Day in the Life of Matthew

Every day with Matthew is an adventure. Some are "excellent", some are not. Most days fall somewhere in between, but somehow, we get through them all one step at a time.

Matthew's typical day begins around 6:30 a.m. School day, or not, he wakes up about the same time. Immediately, he looks for his iPad. We charge it in the kitchen overnight. We have to keep it out of his room just in case he wakes up during the night. If he finds that iPad, he will never go back to sleep! He finds comfort in watching a familiar TV show while taking his medicine and supplements and eating breakfast. Before his attention medications take effect, he is louder than normal and a bit all over the place. He will sing along with the Wiggles or mimic the dreaded Teletubbies while he eats breakfast. Breakfast usually consists of sausage patties, bacon or a biscuit. Occasionally he will eat eggs or cereal.

On school days after breakfast, we make a mad dash to get dressed. He wears a uniform to school, so that makes it a bit easier. However, if I do not check on him and keep him on track, he will forget about getting dressed and get immersed in playing with "the toys from Andy's room" and have them strategically placed throughout his room like a scene from Toy Story 2. He will ask me no less than 10 times, "Why can't I stay home all day?" and insist that he "doesn't want to go to school." After a reminder that we have to go to school and to get dressed quickly, he dresses himself, puts away his dirty clothes and his toys and plays Roblox for a few minutes before we drive to school. Hopefully we remember to put his charged laptop and headphones in his backpack; otherwise I might make an extra trip to SHCS later in the day.

On the way to school, we say our prayers, study any last-minute topics for tests, and then he gets to play on his iPad on the drive to school. If he's playing Word Cookies, I will get asked several times for "one more word." He will give me the letters and the number of letters in the missing word and we will work on the answer. He does not understand that I cannot look at his iPad screen and solve his word problem while driving. Once we reach a certain point in the drop-off line, he puts his iPad in its spot in the car and then asks me, "Who's picking you (meaning him) up today?" He always wants to know, and if he does not, he will likely ask his teacher about a hundred times. He places his headphones on his ears as he exits the car and prepares to face the challenges of the school day. Don't get me wrong—his school embraces Matthew and does everything they can to accommodate his needs. But there are some sensory challenges that can be lessened but not eliminated.

When you ask Matthew why he does not like school the answer is always the same: "there are too many bells." The bells signaling the change of classes are a constant thorn in his side. He wears headphones, non-noise cancelling ones, to muffle the sounds, but they do not prepare him for the surprise of the bells. Even though they ring at the same time every day, the sudden sound ringing through the air unnerves him every time. In addition, he lives in constant fear of a fire drill. The sound of the fire alarm takes his senses to a whole other level and can derail his day. Thankfully, we only have those about once a month. As he moves from class to class, the crowded and noisy halls overwhelm him. He is afraid of being shocked by a passing student in a fleece jacket or by the next bell that can ring at any moment.

Sometimes I get a call to bring the headphones he forgot in the car or a refill of his medication or for just a moment with him on the phone to help him find his calm. He has his people at school that look out for him and do what they can to make his environment more calming, but the reality is that the real world is noisy and crowded and he has to live in that world.

All day he tries to answer questions that come at him quickly or are phrased in a way he might not immediately process. Just when he figures out what is going on in one class, it is time to move to another. He lives in a constant state of sensory overload. Again, these are the basic characteristics of living in the real world, but they are overwhelming for him.

By the time I pick him up, Matthew is ready for a quick debrief and then a break on his iPad. We usually get a snack after school. We are McDonalds most consistent and faithful customers. Matthew's McDonald's order always includes "French fries, chicken and diet coke with no ice." He can order for himself; now he has to learn how to pay for it with the right change. Baby steps.

Matthew will likely ask me why we don't have Playhouse Disney anymore or whether the mail came about ten times until we get home. He might tell me about an incident at school, and if he is sad, he will tell me. "Elephant died."

After school, Matthew does homework (with Mrs. Mommy or Mrs. Robinson) or goes to swim lessons or Speech Therapy (twice a week). There is not a lot of downtime.

Homework is painful. Matthew wants to do anything but more school when he gets home, but "we have to." Some things, like grammar, he flies through. Religion and math require more time and effort, and occasionally tears.

After homework, it's "screen time." One of Matthew's favorite pastimes is to watch one thing on my Mac while listening to or watching another on his iPad. He might play one video, with music from another unrelated show and tape that with his iPad. He is so happy there at the computer, playing, singing, decompressing from all the stressors of his day. Sometimes he sits quietly, while other days he sings so loudly that Walker cannot focus on his own homework.

I'm not sure what triggers the different versions of Matthew. He might ask me to take a picture or to bake a cake or order a movie. He might ask me five hundred times why the lady from Disney never mailed us back explaining why Playhouse Disney is not on TV anymore. Or he might just be, watching television quietly, or building Legos or setting up a feast of plastic food.

Dinner for Matthew consists of one of about five meals he enjoys: pizza or fish sticks or mac and cheese or plain pasta or, on a really adventurous day, grilled salmon. He takes his nighttime medications, finally able to swallow them rather than chewing them up. He will want chocolate milk "filled up to 300." The cup he uses has a 300 ml mark and he prefers his milk filled right up to that line. Then it is bath and bed or just straight to bed. He lets you know it is time for bed around 8:30 or 9:00. He will ask you to put his iPad on charge, in the kitchen, when he is ready. If he is hungry, he will ask for a bag of Cheetos. He will not eat more than one or two before he falls asleep. He will want his stuffed Dalmatian (or BethAnne's). Lately, I have asked him to get the "doll" and bring it to bed himself.

Matthew will talk through the challenges of his day or his world, sometimes simple thoughts and sometimes deeper, harder to explain ones. He likes to fall asleep in "Mrs. Mommy's bed," but on "Dad's side." In his perfect world, Mrs. Mommy lays down when he does and falls asleep there right beside him. The world is not perfect, and more nights than not, Mrs. Mommy (or Dad) moves him to bed after he falls asleep. He sleeps hard until he does not, he snores and he talks in his sleep about the Wiggles, PlayHouse Disney, etc… I cannot imagine how tired he must be. I wonder what it must be like to be him for a day and I wonder if I will ever find out.

The No-Screen Blues

The beginning of Matthew's Sixth grade school year was a little rough for a variety of reasons. He does not love school to begin with: the return to work, decrease in screen time, fire drills, a new teacher to test out. Matthew's wonderful team at Sacred Heart Cathedral met and devised a behavior plan for him.

The first plan involved Matthew writing Mrs. Mommy a letter each time he got in trouble, because he hates having to tell me he is in trouble. This worked for a little while, but the team quickly realized that once he was in trouble and knew he had consequences ahead of him, it was difficult to right the ship. Revision 2 involved a sliding scale of behavior to help him know where he stood. The scale began with "Outstanding" and slid down through the following: Excellent Choices, Great Effort, Ready to Learn, Think About it, Make Better Choices and Parent Contact.

This plan worked but needed to be enforced from class to class, which evolved into Revision 3. This revision, which is still in place, centers around the traditional "Green Light, Yellow Light, Red Light" method. Matthew starts each of his 8 class periods on green light. To get screen time at school or home, he has to have 6 green lights a day and no reds. In the initial days of Revision 3, he had days with lots of yellow. After several months, he rarely had more than one yellow period in a week. One week, he had an entire week of green—YAY!

After school on one of the days of this behavior plan, where he had lost screen time because of a poor choice at school, Matthew experienced great sadness. He suffered from, in his words, the **No Screen Blues**. He sang a song to the tune of *The Higglytown Heroes Ripped Pants Blues*. It broke my heart and also filled me with great joy. I asked him to write the words to his sad song for me. I saved them to share with him.

The No Screen Blues

When I woke up this morning, the sun was in the sky.
   I was playing with my iPad and then mom called me to go to school.
   I made bad choices, I pushed someone and knocked down a chair.
   I can never smile again, because I have the no screen blues.
   My mom said to have a positive attitude but I didn't.
   Now, the TV's turned off and the DVD player is off too
   I have the no screen blues.
   I tried to be careful, I just made one mistake.
   I had pizza for lunch, but then made bad choices in worship.
   Now the computer is off and the iPad is off too. I have the no screen blues.

"Mom, isn't that the saddest song you have ever heard?"

"Definitely one of the saddest songs, Matthew."

Yet, I am not so sad. Matthew is learning there are consequences to his behavior and dealing with the consequences in his own way. He found a way to effectively communicate his despair. He continues to use his favorite episodes or movie scenes to share his emotions. I love his creativity and feel like it's there all of the time just under the surface but is so subtle that I miss it. I am trying to read between the lines more often.

The Backyard

Matthew often keeps quiet on the drive to school, enjoying time on his iPad before he has to focus his efforts on school. One morning he broke the silence,

"Excuse me, Mom, but did you know that the backyard is not only a backyard?"

I said, "No Matthew, what else can the backyard be?"

"Well, sometimes it is a library, with all kinds of books for us to read. Other times it is Paris, with that tower and the fancy museum It. What is that tower called?"

"The Eiffel Tower. What else can the backyard be?" I asked, hoping the dialogue would continue.

"It can be a museum with statues and treasure. It can be a place to go camping with a tent, s'mores, and a sleeping bag. It can be Antarctica where it is very cold with igloos and polar bears. It can be a jungle with trees and vines or rivers and waterfalls. It can be the rain forest with beautiful flowers. It can be the circus with clowns that 'do not make me laugh' and a trapeze person. It can be a soccer field where a player scores a goal."

His continued dialogue shocked me. It's unusual for him to speak on any subject for a long time. I wanted to continue the conversation for as long as he would speak. So, I prompted him with, "What else can our backyard be?"

"Sometimes…the backyard is a beach with hermit crabs and sandcastles. Sometimes…it is the woods with bear hunts and bald eagles. The backyard can be Mexico where the Monarch butterflies migrate. I'm tired. I don't want to explore the backyard anymore."

And just as quickly as it started, it ended. These moments of prolonged conversation are such treasures. I often forget how much like a steel trap his mind is, hurrying him to answer questions or complete his thoughts and then in a moment of clarity, he opens up and shares what's inside and I am reminded just how much is in there. This exchange reminded me a lot of our earlier conversation about dreams and how I must create more opportunities for him to share what's inside, his way, on his terms.

I'm Going Over!

I am not completely sure when Matthew's fascination with waterfalls began. I believe it started with an episode of The Backyardigans where the characters' musical instruments went over a waterfall on a raft. He watched that episode and specifically that part where the instruments went over one by one, over and over and over again. That experience led to him searching for waterfalls on YouTube and watching countless videos of waterfalls and people or things going over them.

This interest in falling water transferred to waterslides and watching people come down them. Matthew still enjoys catching a deep breath and going under water near the spot where someone comes off the waterslide and hits the water. He enjoys throwing things into the water—rocks, sticks, balls, anything—and then waiting for the splash. He loves watching the impact. I have been unsuccessful in getting him to communicate the specifics of his interest or why he likes watching things hit the water. Maybe one day.

While he enjoys watching videos of waterfalls, he enjoys seeing them in person even more. Despite his typical teenage desire to watch his screens and avoid outdoor physical activity, he will brave the elements if it involves seeing a waterfall. On a recent trip to Auburn to visit Peyton, she suggested we go to Chewacla State Park and make the quick hike to the waterfall. We made the short drive from her house to the park and began our hike to see the waterfall, which is actually a dam for a manmade lake, but for our purposes it's a waterfall.

You can actually hear the waterfall before you see it. The sound of the rushing water encouraged Matthew to walk a little faster and when he finally saw it, his face lit up and he headed closer for a better look. Brett and Walker took off with Matthew to explore, while Peyton stayed back to entertain me. I wasn't exactly dressed for hiking! We took some pictures and watched the boys from afar. My blood pressure rose a few times as they let Matthew have a little more "room" to explore than I would prefer. It's amazing how surefooted he was on the rocks; for a child with such weak motor skills, he possesses an amazing sense of balance.

Eventually the boys grew tired of exploring, and Matthew was ready to head back to mom. They chose a different path for their return and it appeared to require a bit of a "jump" across the water. Brett and Walker were on opposite sides of the gap and appeared to be discussing the mechanics of getting Matthew across. Matthew had other plans. He let go of Brett and "attempted" to make the big step across the gap. In slow motion, he missed the step and fell into the cold water. Fortunately, the water was shallow and Walker immediately pulled him out. It easily could be a video submitted for America's Funniest Videos! Matthew came up shouting "Help!" even though he was already saved, while joyfully exclaiming, "I went over the waterfall!" Once we determined that Matthew was fine, we couldn't control our laughter.

Before "going over" (photo credit: Peyton Parra, edited by Kim Bernstein)

After "going over" (photo credit: Peyton Parra, edited by Kim Bernstein)

My next concern was how unhappy Matthew might be on the ride back to Peyton's in his wet clothes and shoes. Once again, he surprised me. He did say he was "all wet," but he didn't complain. He hiked back to the car, entertaining us with the story over and over again, making sure we all knew he "went over the waterfall," smiling with every word. He loved seeing the pictures of his adventure and said he would like to visit that place again, but not get so wet! If I had been the one to go down in the water, I assure you the ride home would not have been so pleasant, I know I would have complained the whole way back, but not a peep out of him. He just wanted to know if he could have "French fries, chicken, coke with no ice." McDonald's is always Matthew's choice to refuel after his great adventures.

[3] The Wiggles. "Georgia's Song." *Go to Sleep Jeff,* KOCH Records, 2003, Track 20, genius.com/The-wiggles-georgias-song-lyrics.

4

"Elephant"

A Hippopotamus for Christmas!

Matthew loves holidays, especially those with cake, but Christmas is his favorite. He kicks off the fall/winter holiday trifecta with Halloween. He picks out a costume and then changes his mind about a dozen times before he finally settles his mind. This year it was an international super spy with a bow tie, a "helicopter" hat and a shirt that buttons. Easy enough!

Then, we roll into (and out of) Thanksgiving and with that special holiday we get cake and days off of school. What's not to like? Soon after, he begins the countdown of sleeps until Christmas, the decorating of the trees, making of lists, and let's not forget the letter to Santa. This year's letter started off simple. Matthew asked for a laptop (check), the stuff to make S'mores (check) and a purple hippo squeaky toy (what?). I did a quick rewind, what exactly is a purple hippo squeaky toy? Matthew explained that Kipper the Dog has a purple hippo squeaky toy and that Santa will bring him one, too.

"Oh", I thought, "a dog toy." Santa can surely handle that! He probably has one in the stock room or can find one at PetLand or on Amazon.

Apparently, Matthew wasn't the only one interested in a purple hippo squeaky toy this year, because while they do exist online, they were all sold out, everywhere, even China. As the number of sleeps until Christmas dwindled, we suggested new ideas of things Santa could bring instead of a purple hippo squeaky toy, but Matthew insisted Santa would bring one. "He can make ANYTHING!"

The day before school let out for the holidays and just nine sleeps until Christmas, I reserved some hours to assist Santa in his search. I went to PetLand, Pet Co and Pet Smart, while they had a variety of animal shaped squeaky toys, none of them were hippos and none of them were purple. I went to Toys'R'Us thinking maybe they would have a stuffed purple hippopotamus that Santa could use. Nope! In a moment of desperation, I headed to the place that everyone tries to avoid at Christmas. No, not the mall—Walmart.

My Walmart adventure started in the pet section, scouring the shelves for a purple hippo. Two older ladies shopping for their animals asked if I needed any help, guessing I looked a little frantic digging through the bins of pet toys. I explained our dilemma and they chuckled and moved on. I know they thought I was crazy and in retrospect, I was a little crazy that day. I was about ready to declare defeat, but I decided to make a quick pass through the toy aisles—just in case. I saw someone who worked in Toys, quickly explained my plight and she said "We did have some stuffed hippos, but I'm pretty sure we sold out. You are welcome to look around. They came in multiple sizes so there could be one around here somewhere." I dug through the bins of the larger animals—giraffes, dolphins, elephants, but no hippos. I began to walk the aisles. Out of the corner of my eye, in the Fisher Price section, I saw a purple, plastic hippo, part of some zoo or safari collection. He was hard and he didn't squeak, but he was a purple hippo. I picked him up and continued to scan the shelves, just in case, when suddenly I saw them. Two-tone purple, plush hippopotamuses, about 4 inches long. I quickly grabbed one to squeeze it and see if it would squeak. No squeak—but it was a purple hippopotamus and it could be squeezed. I grabbed two of them. Anyone with a child on the spectrum will understand why.

My mind began to race and a plan formed. I headed back across the store to the pet section in search of the smallest squeaky ball I could lay my hands on. As soon as I found the balls, I reached for my phone and called the "Grand" Elf. I needed hippo transplant surgery and I knew she was just the one to perform the surgery. After checking out with 3 purple hippos and two squeaky balls, I headed to Grand's. The "Grand" Elf assured me, "Of course, I can perform a transplant on a purple hippo toy and when he wakes up he will be a purple hippo squeaky toy."

Fast forward nine sleeps and it's Christmas Morning. Matthew ran into the game room to see what Santa left for him. Santa did well, He left a laptop, chocolate bars, graham crackers, marshmallows and a purple hippo squeaky toy. Matthew carried that hippo around all day, squeaking him every so often. He said. "Santa did a great job this year!" That compliment, my friends, is worth all the effort!

An Elephant Update

Over one Thanksgiving holiday we traveled to Houston to visit BethAnne at Rice. That Saturday, she needed some chauffeuring around town to different printers to complete an architecture project. While we were in one of the stores, Peyton and Walker decided to take Matthew to a pet store to pass the time. Seemed like a good idea…

They meandered up and down the aisles looking at fish, kittens, reptiles, until they reached the hamsters. Matthew quickly fixated on the hamsters and wanted to buy one. That day. They aborted the mission and headed to the car with a tearful Matthew. When BethAnne and I returned to the car several minutes later, we met tears…I think all of them were tearful: Brett, Peyton, Walker and Matthew, over Matthew's somber requests to get a hamster.

Peyton and Walker quickly brought me up to speed. Peyton explained that Matthew went so far as to try to find "thirty-five dollars" in her wallet, so he could buy that hamster!!

Mrs. Mommy went into master negotiator mode. I wanted to save the day, for all of us. Racking my brain for something that would redirect Matthew, I began to offer up ideas of different treats: a new DVD, McDonald's French fries, chicken and Coke with no ice, anything to change the downward spiral we were facing. Suddenly I remembered that on a recent Target visit I saw a little "electronic" hamster in the toy department. I asked Matthew if we could get a pretend hamster?

He thought for a minute, took a deep breath and said "Yes!" Brett immediately mapped the nearest Target and we headed that way. Once there, Matthew led us to the toy department and picked out a hamster. Crisis averted!

Back in Pensacola the following week, I asked Matthew to work on a letter to Santa. He told me, in no uncertain terms, he wanted a "hamster, a real one, not a toy, not one with batteries."

Ugh! A rodent? "I don't know if Santa brings hamsters," I said.

Matthew thought for a minute and said, "He will."

I had no words. I shared our conversation with Brett that night and Brett was as reluctant as I was. Over the next few days, we talked about hamsters a lot. We started to research them and, in the meantime, I tried to encourage Matthew to think of other things Santa might bring if he couldn't find a hamster.

On Sunday evening, our neighborhood hosted a Christmas gathering, and Santa and Mrs. Claus arrived in the back of a pickup truck. Matthew and I made a beeline to see them. Matthew was in a bit of a moody state that night and I should have known maybe this wasn't the best time to speak with Santa. However, I also wanted him to have the experience of Santa, up close and personal. Matthew walked up to Santa and exclaimed, "I want a hamster, a live one!"

Santa looked at Matthew and then at me and responded, "Santa doesn't bring live animals!"

I could see this wasn't going to end well. The tears started, and Matthew walked away, heartbroken. Mrs. Claus, the brains behind the operation, approached me and asked how we could salvage this. I quickly explained our situation; she suggested another visit with Santa in a few minutes after she briefed him. I convinced Matthew to give it another try, He was adamantly opposed, but I bribed him with a cookie. (Yes, I do resort to bribes.)

Matthew patiently—well, kind of patiently—waited to talk to Santa. When it was his turn, Matthew went to Santa and made his case for "Elephant!" You see, Matthew wanted a hamster because of Little Bill. Little Bill on Nick, Jr. had a hamster named "Elephant," and Matthew loved Little Bill. Little Bill has lots of fun with Elephant, so we would have fun with one too! Right?

Negotiating with Santa (photo credit: Mrs. Mommy, edited by Kim Bernstein)

Well of course, I was a puddle after watching Matthew make his case for Elephant with Santa. His negotiations with Santa convinced me to write my own letter. Santa listened, did his own research and delivered a long haired, Syrian male hamster to Matthew on Christmas morning.

Matthew likes to take his hamster out and put him in the hamster ball, always without telling me. So, I sometimes get the benefit of walking into the office and finding an empty hamster cage. Usually there is a moment of immense panic that our cat Chai has finally figured out how to get the weights off the lid and has treated herself to afternoon snack. Chai sits next to the cage for hours watching the hamster and contemplating his demise! However, that panic is always met with relief when Matthew turns around with a big smile and hands me the hamster ball with Elephant in it, saying, "I need to ask for help first!" And that, folks, is the story of how we came to own a hamster named "Elephant."

H is for Hamster, Hippopotamus and Hermit Crab

Matthew's fascination with letters and words began at an early age. He loved the PBS television show Word World and from there learned to spell words fairly easily. I remember a family car trip when he was quite young and with limited conversational speech, he said "d-o-g, that spells dog." I asked him what else he could spell. He said, "c-a-t, that spells cat and c-a-k-e, that spells cake and t-r-a-i-n s-t-a-t-i-on- that spells train station." We were all dumbfounded and couldn't believe our ears. We asked where he learned to spell like that and he said, "Word World." PBS to the rescue.

Moose and Zee from Noggin taught Matthew another exercise he enjoys. Starting with A at the beginning of the alphabet, first he asks "What are your favorite words that start with the letter A?" and then he lists all the things he can think of that start with that letter, Then he goes to the next letter. Sometimes, if he runs out of words before he is ready to move on to the next letter, he lets me join in. Other times, he says, "Don't do it Mom, I can do it myself!"

I often ask him why he likes this game so much and he simply says, "Because it's fun!"

My favorite letter to join in on is H, because H is for Hamster, Hippopotamus and Hermit Crab.

It has amazed me how long we have had Matthew's hamster, "Elephant." He tries to escape his cage on a regular basis by climbing on top of his water bottle and trying to push the top of the cage off! He got so close to success that we had to put a weight on top of the cage to keep him in. A big shout out to our friends that recommended we keep him in an aquarium with a wire top instead of a traditional "rodent" plastic cage with lots of openings. It is much easier cleanup and less odor and likely less opportunity for a breakout!

You've already read about our second H—the hippopotamus from Christmas. We know that lots of things, good and bad, come in threes, and our third H was for Hermit Crab.

Brett, Walker and I travelled to a swim meet in Auburn, Alabama and unfortunately, both Matthew and Grand were under the weather when we left. Grand rallied and began to feel better, but Matthew's illness lingered a bit.

On that Saturday, Matthew told Grand that he knew something that would make him feel better. She asked, "What?"

He replied, "A hermit crab."

So Grand and Matthew loaded up the car and headed to the beach to Alvin's Island in search of a hermit crab. Guess what? They found one with a blue shell and brought him home. We arrived home late Sunday night to a happy boy with a new pet. As if a dog, cat, and hamster weren't enough, now we also had a hermit crab. Frankly, I did not give the hermit crab a week to survive. I should have known better.

Snappy was still going strong almost two months later. Matthew (and Brett) grew attached to the little fella rather quickly. Brett did some research on what crabs can eat in "captivity" and how best to keep them alive. Apparently, a little water in the cage every few days and some apple slices make for a happy hermit crab. A few weeks ago, when Snappy appeared to be slowing down and not looking so healthy, they decided he might be outgrowing his shell and need a new one. We just happened to have a few shells of different sizes laying around, so Brett and Matthew placed two of them in the cage with the crab. A day or so later, I noticed that the blue shell was empty and Snappy had selected his new home. As much as I hate to admit it, he is a pretty cool pet. Easy to care for and fun to watch. What's your favorite word that starts with the letter H?

"Elephant Died!"

Elephant joined our family in December of 2015 and lasted longer than I thought he would. He survived an escape enabled by Matthew when he let him out of the aquarium and put him in the dog crate. The crate holes were a little too big to contain the hamster; thankfully, an assist from Peyton allowed us to catch him before he escaped through the laundry duct. He survived living in the house with a cat and a dog. The cat spent hours sitting outside the cage just watching, trying to figure a way in. No such luck. Elephant tried to escape his quarters on a routine basis. He lived in a glass aquarium with a wire lid. He would climb on top of the water bottle and try to push the lid off. He was no match for the Parras; we put a weight on top of the cage and squashed the escape plans.

Matthew loved Elephant. He did not always pay attention to him—it came in phases—but he always loved him. He read to him on occasion. He liked to place him in the plastic ball and let him roll around the laundry room. I had a bit of a love/hate relationship with him. He was kind of cute, but still a rodent at the end of the day. My least favorite Elephant duty was cage cleaning. Hamsters make a big mess and poop, often, in case you have never had the pleasure of caring for one.

On November 30, 2017, the night before Matthew's thirteenth birthday, I was working in the office and noticed that Elephant's water bottle appeared just as full as the day before, the food bowl pretty full, and he was "sleeping" in his little plastic igloo. Usually, I could see his body heaving as he slept, but not that night. My heart sank and I called in reinforcements. I was too chicken to take a look myself, so I called "the doctor" to come check it out. As soon as Brett lifted the igloo out of the cage, I knew Elephant was gone.

I suspected that Matthew would be sad and that he would have lots of questions. The only other death he had any experience with was when our German Short Hair Pointer, Ellie, died and he did not seem too phased by that at the time. I DID NOT want to tell him his beloved Elephant had died on his birthday, so I swore Brett and Walker to secrecy. We made a pact to tell him on December 2, the day after his birthday, unless he asked before then. I held my breath much of his birthday, but fortunately he did not ask.

On Saturday morning, when Matthew woke up, we broke the news. Brett and I told him we had some sad news and that Elephant had died. He asked "why" and we explained that he was old in hamster years and must have gotten sick. He asked where he was now and we told him in Animal Heaven. He took it amazingly well and then went back to playing on the computer.

Over the next few days, he began to ask more questions about Elephant's death. He wanted to know why we couldn't take him to the doctor and get him fixed. He cried real tears; it is very unusual for him to cry so earnestly. He told us he wanted Elephant to come back, he wanted "God to trade one of our still-living pets (dog and cat) for Elephant." We tried to explain that it does not work that way and that we do not get to choose when pets (or people) die.

The following week, we went on a field trip with his class. I drove Matthew, his teacher, and four other students. On the way to the movie, Matthew explained to his teacher that his hamster died. He then went on to talk about all of our other pets that have died over the years, Ellie, Annie (a cat we have not had for many years), a hermit crab named Snappy, a goldfish named Brake-O and another goldfish, Goldy. With the exception of Ellie and Snappy, the other pets were around when he was much younger and not nearly as verbal as he is today. We did not realize he had any kind of relationship or active memory of them, but apparently, he did.

That sadness he feels is so real that he uses it as a reference for that feeling when he cannot otherwise find the words. When he is sad about the end of a vacation or losing a privilege or the missing Playhouse Disney Channel series, he will say "Elephant died," with his eyes full of tears and then try to tell us what is making him sad in that moment. We know when he starts with "Elephant died," it is real and heartfelt sadness he is experiencing, and we do what we can to comfort him. How his mind works is such a mystery to me, but there is joy in the unraveling.

5

"One More Word, Please"

Echolalia - The "foundation" of speech
"The National Science Foundation, The Corporation for Public Broadcasting, The Arthur Vining Davis Foundations, The Wieeze Foundation, The Tucker Gosnell Family Foundation, The Met Life Foundation, The Rose Hills Foundation, The S.D. Bechtel, Jr. Foundation, The John W. Carson Foundation, The J.P.B. Foundation and contributions from viewers like you, Thank you!" I can't tell you how many times Matthew has repeated this string of names to me over the past seven years, forwards, backwards, in this order, and so on. They roll off his tongue so comfortably, like the names of old friends.

Echolalia 1. Psychiatry. the uncontrollable and immediate repetition of words spoken by another person. 2.the imitation by a baby of the vocal sounds produced by others, occurring as a natural phase of childhood development[4].

At fifteen months old, Matthew spoke about ten words, typical baby talk: mama, dada, hi, juice, etc. Between fifteen and eighteen months, he lost his voice and his words. His regression, or lack of progression, began. The rollercoaster of figuring out why (and what we were to do about it) left me with whiplash. Speech Therapy at McMillan Elementary became part of our weekly routine (three times per week). Over the next two years, in conjunction with speech and seizure control, Matthew's speech improved.

Matthew began to repeat things, sometimes functionally as part of therapy. More often, he echoed parts of TV shows and movies. Initially, some professionals discouraged his use of echolalia and told us we should do the same. We were conflicted, glad to hear he could speak. We did not want to send a mixed message to Matthew: "We want you to talk, but only the way we say to!"

We created our own name for echolalia: movie talk. We compromised. We discouraged the use of "movie talk" at school and therapy, but allowed him to use it at home.

Over time, we noticed some nuances within the "movie talk." We found that he properly pronounced sounds via echolalia that he could not pronounce when using his own words. We noticed that echolalia appeared when he needed comfort or calm. Most importantly, we discovered that he began to use pieces of his "movie talk" appropriately during conversation.

I decided to research the topic a little further. The reviews were inconsistent. Some professionals encouraged the use of echolalia, while others prohibited it. Then one day on NPR, I heard an author, Ron Suskind (and father of an autistic son) speak about his newly released book *Life, Animated: A Story of Sidekicks, Heroes, and Autism*. This family used his son's love of Disney movies to teach him speech and language, emotions, and social skills. I immediately ordered the book and could not put it down. I saw so many similarities between Matthew and Owen. I laughed out loud on one page and cried crocodile tears the next. I finished the book feeling like, we too, could use "movie talk" to Matthew's advantage.

Earlier that month, I had told Matthew about my writing. I explained that I wrote stories about him and our family and autism. I asked for his permission to share these stories and he said, "Sure." I went on to ask what I should write about.

One of the things he wanted me to write about were the "foundations." I pressed and asked why. He replied that "they make me happy; the foundations make me happy." Probably because some of his favorite PBS television shows are "provided by" these foundations. So subtle, yet so wise. I, too, am grateful for the "foundations," because they helped my sweet Matthew find his voice.

Those who know Matthew know when he uses his own words and when he borrows them from someone else. When you know the lines he borrows, you are blessed, because for a moment (or an hour), you step into his world and you share his words. He speaks one line, you speak the next. You feel his joy, you make a connection, and it stays with you, long after the moment passes.

Movie Talk

Last night, Brett, Walker and I watched the documentary *Life, Animated,* based on the book *Life, Animated: A Story of Sidekicks, Heroes, and Autism.* I am not sure I can do justice to the emotions I experienced watching the movie. The documentary chronicles a brief window of Owen and his family's life experience, as compared to the book which covers his life from diagnosis to present day.

Matthew loves animated movies and television, specifically anything Disney Pixar. He is well-rounded enough that he includes features from PBS, Sprout, Noggin, Hit Entertainment and Nick, Jr., but Disney Pixar never falls out of favor. It is such a part of who he is and his everyday speech, that we began to refer to his use of movie dialogue as "movie talk." For quite some time, we discouraged his "movie talk" because we didn't know or understand that he might be using these words, phrases, scenes and episodes to communicate with us. Brett and I recognized at times that he was using phrases from movies appropriately in conversation and that if the person he was speaking to wasn't familiar with the script, they might never know.

When I read Suskind's book the first time, I immediately felt a connection to Owen and his family. There were certain passages where I felt as if I were reading about Matthew. I share the book with family, teachers, and therapists whenever possible. I hope it provides them with another perspective or insight that opens their mind to ways to reach Matthew.

The movie, which stars Owen, his parents and his older brother Walt, is equally stirring. I believe that almost anyone who parents, teaches, works with or loves someone autistic would benefit from screening the movie. Watching Owen's parents share their hopes and fears for him was unsettling, because we share many of those same sentiments for Matthew. Seeing his older brother Walt grapple with the impending responsibilities of caring for aging parents and an autistic brother made me wonder about the thoughts and fears BethAnne, Peyton and Walker must experience.

In the movie, Owen is 23 (about 10 years older than Matthew) and I see so much of Matthew in this young autistic man. Watching Owen experience life as an "independent" young adult makes me laugh and moves me to tears. Some of the scenes might be found in any twenty-three-year old's world, while others are unique to Owen. I find myself wanting to meet and befriend his mom, to seek her guidance and advice. I love how his father just met him where he was with an Iago puppet and slowly helped him find his voice through his passion. Ultimately, the family uses Owen's passion for animated sidekicks to help him navigate and understand the world; Owen hypothesizes that others with autism do the same thing with their passions, whether those passions be superheroes or Jewish comedians or Disney sidekicks.

I am on a mission to find the path that helps Matthew become the best version of himself and use his passions (whatever they may be) to help him navigate the world, and this peek into another family's journey was both comforting and timely. If you know and love someone autistic, if you work with autistic people, if you are just curious, rent the movie or read the book or both. I hope you will feel your investment of time and money were worthwhile and that you discover new insights about the autism spectrum disorder.

"Better Words"

One winter break, I decided that Matthew and I would read Harry Potter and the Sorcerer's Stone together in preparation for a summer trip to Universal Studios. We were tagging along with Brett to one of his medical conferences. I thought Matthew might appreciate the park more if he were familiar with some of the characters. I was trying to apply the "read the book before you see the movie" approach that we had used with our older kids.

We read one of the new illustrated versions. If you have not checked them out, you should. They have all the fabulousness of the originals with a few pictures thrown in for good measure. The illustrations are spot on and bring the characters to life just as you might imagine them. Matthew enjoyed meeting Harry and Hagrid and had disdain for the Dursleys just like the rest of us, especially that dreadful Dudley. We were rocking right along, making progress all the way to Chapter Six, "The Journey from Platform Nine and Three Quarters," when something interesting occurred. Page 87, second paragraph: "Sunshine, daisies, butter mellow, Turn this stupid fat rat yellow."

"Mom, stop reading that bad word! We have to change it!"

"Matthew, what bad word?"

"Stupid, we don't say that word. We need to change it to silly! That's a better word."

So, for the first time ever, we took a pen, scratched out a bad word and wrote a new one in its place. We continued to read and on the very next page, "Stupid spell…"

"Mom, stop! They did it again. Another bad word, we have to change it to a better one!"

So again, we changed the word to silly and continued to read. I am intrigued by how his mind works. There are bad words (the ones most teenagers know, but he doesn't thankfully) and then there are BAD words like stupid, shut-up, idiot and moron. Words that Pixar and Nick, Jr., and J.K. Rowling can use, but Matthew and Mrs. Mommy cannot. We've worked tirelessly to keep the bad and hurtful words out of his vocabulary. It, for the most part, has worked. Occasionally when he is really frustrated or angry, he will tell me or Brett that "we don't say idiot or moron or stupid like Pixar." Letting you know he wants to say it, but not calling you by the name. In general, he does not use these words and he does not tolerate other people using them. Try saying one of them in front of him and he will correct you. Sometimes that does not work well for him when the person saying the word is a teacher or parent or another respected adult. He is right though; we can find better words. Just like Matthew takes the pen and literally changes the word in his book, we need to strike the words from our vocabulary and find better ones, kinder ones, more creative ones. Oh, the lessons I continue to learn from Matthew.

"Just one more word please?"

Puzzles always fascinated Matthew, from the chunky wooden ones with handles he "solved" as a toddler to the five hundred-piece ones we work on during Thanksgiving break at Watercolor. Sometimes he turns the pieces over and solves using the shape instead of the colors. Over time this interest expanded to include other problem-solving games, like the Can You Escape game and word puzzles.

The Can You Escape Game involves finding hidden clues that help the user move throughout rooms of a house or museum or cruise ship and so on. You have to find keys to open locks or tools to make a piece of equipment work or use a series of numbers to unlock an elevator or safe. I, frankly, am terrible at it and can never remember where the obscure tool is that holds the "key" to opening the hidden door leading to the treasure. Matthew, in contrast, remembers all the little details, the shape combinations, the intricate number patterns, where to find the pick to open the safe. This game can entertain him for hours.

This year Matthew's teachers introduced him to some word games: "Word Cookies," "Word Shops" and "Word Spinning." Unbeknownst to me, he downloaded the free versions on his iPad and began playing them at home. He blazed through the lower levels without asking for any help, probably because he had already completed them once at school. One day he said, "I just need one more word, please," and shoved his iPad in my direction. I explained that I could not look while driving, but I would take a look when we stopped. Once at our destination, he repeated, "I need one more word, please," and handed me the iPad. Interestingly, he already solved all of the harder words and had one three letter word left. I filled it in and mentally moved on.

As time and his levels have progressed, our solving process has evolved.

He tries to solve the hardest, typically the longest word first, and works backward from there. He will do all he can and then say, "I need one (or two or three) more words, please." Now, I ask, "How many letters," and "What are the letters?" It works well, and we are usually able to complete the task. As the words become more difficult, they often are words that Matthew is not familiar with. He will ask what the words mean and I will try to explain on his level and use the word in a sentence to give him context.

On a college road trip, we got Dad and Walker in on the fun, Dad is really good at this game and Matthew takes the extra challenging words to him. Walker helps when he's not sleeping. (He sleeps a lot on road trips.) I am grateful to Matthew's teachers for introducing him to these games. It is a more productive and educational way for him to spend his "screen" time and it's expanding his vocabulary every day. If you have an affinity for word games or just want to have some fun, download "Word Cookies." I hope you enjoy it as much as we have.

Disgusting Words

When Matthew was younger, he developed a fascination with animal waste, in other words, poop! He would point out the brown stuff to me whenever and wherever he saw it and I would say, "Don't touch that, it's yucky!" He thought the name of it was actually "yucky," not that "yucky" was an adjective or descriptive word.

Somewhere along the way, he began to think of yucky as equivalent to the word "sh**" and therefore as a bad word. (He has heard me say that is a bad word and we should not say it!) As a result, he corrects people when he hears them say either word.

Lately, his aversion to the word yucky has grown and he responds to it much like he does to fire. Twice in a short amount of time he got very worked up when an adult used the word appropriately. The first time was with his teacher Ms. L. and she was redirecting him from picking his nose, which is yucky, while waiting for carline. He climbed into the car very upset because Ms. L was saying disgusting words. I asked him what word and he wouldn't say it, she walked up to the car and explained. I was able to give her a quick explanation of his aversion and tried to explain to him why people use the word and that it doesn't actually refer to poop, no luck; in his mind it will forever refer to poop.

A few months later, Brett said something was yucky. Of course, when he said the word he did not think of Matthew's aversion to the word, so he was shocked when Matthew yelled at him, "Dad, don't say disgusting words!" This prompted a discussion at first between Brett and Matthew about disgusting words, which was followed by a translation by me of why and how we got to yucky equaling sh**! Brett had an aha moment of why we don't say yucky and Matthew chimed in from the backseat with a sassy, "Dad, don't say disgusting words anymore, just stop talking and focus on driving!" You can only imagine the looks on our faces, teenage sass at its finest. Thank goodness Matthew could not see our faces!

[4] Dictionary.com

6

The Magic of Disney

"Our Friends" at Disney Pixar

From the very beginning, before autism was a household word for us, Matthew loved Disney Pixar, and his diagnosis certainly did not affect that love. Any Disney Pixar movie holds his attention for at least several viewings, but some of them can be watched several times a day, for weeks, months, and years. Certain movies and characters became such a part of our lives, they are like old friends: comfortable, trustworthy, and always there when you need them, even at 2:00 am when insomnia strikes. *Cars, Frozen, Finding Nemo, Up*, and *Brave* are in the rotation. But the all-time favorite, the one we cannot leave home without, is the *Toy Story* series: *Toy Story, Toy Story 2, Toy Story 3, Toy Story that Time Forgot* and *Toy Story of Terror*. Buzz and Woody are Matthew's constant companions. They traveled to Alaska, Maine, and Wyoming. They sat though countless hours of swim meets, basketball games, and awards ceremonies.

Matthew has learned valuable lessons from "our friends" (his words, not mine). He sometimes uses these lessons and their related scripts to apply to situations in his world. Several years of scripting passed before Brett and I realized that his scripting—repeating scenes word for word from a movie or TV show—might just be for comfort or his way of trying to tell us something or to communicate his feelings when he could not find his own words. It really sank in one day last year as Matthew asked Walker to "play" with him.

Matthew pulled out a cardboard box with all the *Toy Story* friends in it and Matthew scripted Andy's words and instructed Walker to be Bonnie. He "acted" out the final scene of *Toy Story 3* where Andy gives Bonnie his *Toy Story* friends over and over again. The constant was Matthew as Andy and whoever he could get to stand in was Bonnie.

It perplexed me. Why act out this particular scene at this particular time? In a moment of clarity, I realized that Matthew had been silently listening and processing hours of conversation about college over the previous year and a half. As BethAnne prepared to apply to college and ultimately go away to college, we spoke about it for countless hours in front of Matthew, but not to Matthew. I realized it was time to talk with him about NaNa, (his name for her) going to college and explain that while BethAnne would go away to college, she would also come home again. Matthew filed his "going to college" script away for a few years and pulled it out as Peyton and then Walker left for college. It's like the movie scenes he finds comfort in are organized in some emotionally-driven fashion, and he refers back to them for help processing thoughts or feelings he finds otherwise difficult to express. I hope that one day he can explain his filing system to me.

The Claw

I believe Matthew's fascination with "the claw" began years ago watching *Toy Story*. In that movie, there is a scene at Pizza Planet in which Buzz climbs into the claw machine thinking it is a spaceship. Woody follows him trying to avert a crisis. Unfortunately, Woody's efforts are in vain, and Buzz and Woody end up in Sid's laboratory, a place few toys escape! At one point in the scene, the little green aliens say in unison, "The claw!" When Matthew spoke few words, but lived and breathed all things *Toy Story*, he would line his aliens up with Buzz and Woody and say, "the claw," over and over again.

Over time, I forgot his interest in this scene, because he rotated from one movie to a specific episode of a television show to a different movie and then back again. There is an episode of *Wow Wow Wubbzy* (not my favorite) where Wubbzy plays the grabbity grab game to win a prize. Unlike *Toy Story*, which

I watched at least one-hundred times in the past 12 years, I never actually watched this episode of Wubbzy. If I had, I would have known the grabbity grab game was just Nickelodeon's way of saying "the claw." I might have made the connection.

Then in 2010, Pixar re-introduced "the claw" in the final heart-wrenching scene of *Toy Story 3*. (No spoilers from me. If you have not seen it, run, do not walk, to the RedBox and rent it. You will not be disappointed—it is beautiful. One of the best sequel movies ever.) When *Toy Story 3* finally released to DVD, he watched this claw scene over and over again. Total reinvention of the claw, but a throwback to the original in the way only Disney Pixar can.

A few years later, Matthew saw a claw machine game in person Brett and Walker "won" a ball for Matthew. We definitely spent more money than the ball cost, but we had fun, and Matthew had a new interest. He began to notice claw machine games everywhere: Wal-Mart, the movie theatre, Golden Corral and SkyZone. He created a pretend claw machine game at home with kitchen tongs and lots of small plush toys. We all "won" playing Matthew's version. I decided that trips to the claw machine might be great motivation for good behavior at school, completing homework in a timely and cooperative manner, letting the barber use clippers during a haircut. And it worked, well—really well.

I could not put my finger on where this fascination came from—was it the chance to "win?" Was it watching the machine work? Was it because of a movie? After speculating for too long, I simply asked Matthew, "Why do you like the claw machine game? Is it from a movie or television show?"

He looked at me, like really looked at me, like I was a crazy person and matter-of-factly replied, "It's fun." Duh! He paused and continued, "It's from the *Toy Story* and *Wubbzy*."

Instantly, I remembered the *Toy Story* scene, but he had to show me the *Wubbzy* episode. Pixar's use is infinitely more creative and less annoying. I continue to be perplexed by how he applies things he watches in movies or TV shows to life. I would love to know why certain scenes and characters resonate with him and bring him joy, while others garner no interest.

In the meantime, we will play the claw game as a reward. He recently led me to the "room" at Wal-Mart where they have FIVE machines. He walked right up to the one with the plush toy he planned to win and asked me to help. No pressure, right? I am happy to report that we won the toy of choice on our last attempt. He looked at me like I was a super hero and I almost cried. Then he said, "I'm done. Let's go to Speech."

The Toys from Andy's Room

Buzz and Woody have been constant in Matthew's life and, by extension, our family life as well. Both *Toy Story* and *Toy Story 2* were released years before Matthew was born, and I don't recall exactly how or when we introduced him to the gang. But I'm sure they became fast friends upon first introduction because I do not remember a time when they were not Matthew's favorites.

Unless you are a Pixar aficionado, I bet you did not know that there are different versions of Buzz and Woody to go with each movie. Matthew knows, and he has favorites. Buzz Lightyear with the blue utility belt is at the top of the list. He can spot a Buzz impersonator from a mile away. No, they don't make "Blue Belt Buzz" anymore and yes, I have spent entirely too much money replacing him, once or twice or three times. Fortunately, eBay sellers from England do not always appreciate the popularity of Utility Belt Buzz in the United States, so sometimes you can get a deal from across the pond.

While Buzz and Woody are the most significant in Matthew's mind, you can find the rest of the gang in his room as well: Rex, Ham, Jesse, Slinky Dog, the Prospector, Lotso, Wheezy and, of course, Bullseye. These toys are well traveled; they have been to Maine, Massachusetts, Alaska, Utah, Colorado, Mexico, Louisiana, Mississippi, Alabama, Georgia and, most recently, Texas.

Before a trip, Matthew carefully selects who gets to accompany Buzz and Woody on the next adventure. He's even carried Buzz Lightyear all over Disney World.

These toys do not sit on the shelf and gather dust. Matthew plays with them, he experiments with them, he reenacts scenes from movies in method, he takes them apart and tries to put them back together. He "learned" to use a screwdriver after *Toy Story 3*'s 2010 release because he wanted to see if Buzz really had a switch on his back that changed his language of choice to Spanish! He recreates different scenes from the movies and his creativity shines.

One day, Brett found a trashcan with miscellaneous toys, hundreds of Lego mini figure arms and a Woody doll. I knew it was the "nightmare" scene of broken-armed Woody. Needless to say, we did not "trash" any toys. Matthew used the final scene from *Toy Story 3* where Andy gifts the toys to Bonnie before going to college to help him process his sisters going to college. Sometimes he sings with the gang, "You've Got a Friend in Me" or "The Toys are Back in Town" or "When Somebody Loves You." I will sneak up and just listen to him serenade them. It fills my heart.

I realized that there are only figures for the toys from these movies, none of the people characters are represented in figurine form. No Andy, No Al, No Bonnie… Matthew recently asked for an Andy doll and I explained there wasn't one. His reply was, "Why not?" I honestly did not know. If I ever had the chance to meet John Lassiter (or the three other creators) I would ask him this question and then I would profusely thank him for the gang from Andy's Room and tell him how the "friends" eased some of the difficult moments for Matthew, how they accompanied Matthew to EEGs, and certain nights they made sleep come easier. Most importantly, their timeless nature is such a complement to my sweet boy who is a bit like Peter Pan.

The Toys from Andy's Room (photo credit: Mrs. Mommy, edited by Kim Bernstein)

Buzz and Woody are old and faithful friends. They have been around as long as he can remember. They do not outgrow him, like "real" boys and girls and he will not outgrow them. (Maybe that is why they do not make toy versions of the people characters, people grow up and move on.) These friends do not ask for much in return, just love and attention. They will follow wherever he goes and he can always count on them. In a changing and sometimes overwhelming world, they provide comfort and routine. I asked him tonight, "Why are Buzz and Woody your favorites? Why do you always come back to them?" and he said, "Because they make me happy and they are are my friends!"

The Happiest Place on Earth

Disney World continues to be a favorite vacation destination for our family for a multitude of reasons: we share lots of happy memories there, Disney truly welcomes families with special needs, and it's the "happiest place on Earth!" One summer, Brett, BethAnne, Matthew and I visited Disney. Well, Brett went to his annual Florida Medical Association meeting and BethAnne, Matthew and I visited a few Disney parks.

BethAnne serves as our Disney travel planner. She helps me identify restaurants and shows Matthew might enjoy. I am grateful for her help and amazed by her knowledge of all things Disney.

During this visit, we visited EPCOT first, because Matthew likes it least. We built up to visiting the parks he would enjoy more later in the trip. The adults enjoyed eating our way around the countries. Matthew was not so impressed, as there were not enough opportunities for French fries and chicken and Diet Coke with no ice.

On our second day we visited Hollywood Studios, Matthew's favorite. There was Playhouse Disney, now called Disney, Jr.—much to Matthew's chagrin. There was Toy Story Mania, we used his disability access pass, over and over and over again, so he could play the Toy Story themed carnival games. We survived waiting in line for about an hour to see Buzz and Woody (you cannot use disability pass for this) only to find that Buzz was on a "bathroom break". Amazingly, Matthew said, "maybe next time" and smiled for his picture with Woody. We also enjoyed a special limited performance at the Beauty and the Beast Theatre of *The Music of Pixar Live! A Symphony of Characters*. An orchestra performed some Pixar favorites while accompanied by beloved characters like the Incredibles, Nemo and Dory and Buzz Lightyear and Woody. Matthew loved every second of it. He even sang along with "You've Got a Friend."

We also celebrated the end of an iconic attraction-*The Great Movie Ride*—well some of us did. BethAnne wanted to make sure we went on the ride one last time before it was shuttered later in the summer. When we were talking about it, Matthew keep insisting that he "did not want to go on the Mary Poppins ride." We did not know what he was talking about and told him, we were going on the *The Great Movie Ride* before it was converted to *Mickey & Minnie's Runaway Railway*. He continued to insist, "No Mary Poppins!"

When we walked up to the ride, guess what we found? Mary Poppins! The front right display window entering the line to the ride featured memorabilia from the Mary Poppins movie! One more example of Matthew's amazing memory and how we should be certain that if he claims to see something or hear something, it is there! Matthew finally agreed to go on the ride one last time.

During our third day we explored Magic Kingdom until our feet wore out and the crowds became too much. We did not leave without hitting Matthew's favorites: *Buzz Lightyear's Space Ranger Spin*, *Splash Mountain* (thanks dad and BethAnne!), *It's a Small World* and *Snow White's Mine Train*. We ate a yummy breakfast in the *Beauty and the Beast* castle. For most of the trip, Matthew passed on buying treats, saving his money to buy a "Zurg Blaster" outside of the Buzz Lightyear ride. He wanted to purchase it the previous year, but I said it was "too big." This year, he was willing to pool his money and buy that one toy. He entered the store, walked straight to the spot the toy was located the previous year only to find it had been replaced by a new model. He was dejected that the green Zurg blaster was gone, and he didn't want the new one. Ugh, what was a mom to do? Amazon to the rescue! Some quick thinking led Mrs. Mommy to do an Amazon search while in the store. Sure enough, the old model was available and would arrive in Pensacola about the same time we did! He was happy to have the toy he imagined en route and I was happy I did not have to carry it around the park all day! A win-win!

We do not say farewell when we leave Disney; we instead use the words of Mickey Mouse: "See you real soon!" While we outgrow many things from our childhoods, we do not outgrow Disney World. When we walk through those famous gates, it brings out the inner child in all of us.

7

"Get Jesus"

Answered Prayers

Brett and I have known each other for over thirty years. We married during his third year of medical school and my senior year of college. We sort of grew up together, started our careers, and prepared to start a family. Only the family planning didn't initially go quite as we hoped. After a few years and no pregnancies, we decided to seek professional help! We learned that I suffered from PCOS (polycystic ovary syndrome), which complicated our ability to get pregnant.

It was a very difficult time for us. Brett worked non-stop, with call every third night in residency, and I worked as a CPA, first for a "big six" firm and then for a local hospital. We both wanted to be parents. Most of our peers were new parents or expecting their first child or second child, but it just wasn't happening for us. Everyone asked, "Are you trying to have a baby?" or "Why don't you have children?" or "Are you going to be a career woman with no kids?" I answered as best I could, while trying to maintain some privacy.

We decided to see a specialist, and he recommended medication and monitoring of my "levels". We proceeded. The medication and hormones, put me on a bit of an emotional roller coaster. I cried over anything. One night, I decided to cook dinner for Brett, who was on the transplant service at the time. I prepared a venison recipe in a Pyrex dish. I, incorrectly, assumed that Pyrex was stovetop safe because it was oven safe. (Let's just say that my cooking skills have progressed since then.) Brett walked in the door about two minutes after the Pyrex dish exploded and venison gravy adorned every surface in the kitchen. I was a puddle of tears. He laughed; I cried some more. Just as we started to clean up, his beeper sounded and he headed to the airport for an organ harvest in Miami leaving me to my mess. I can laugh about it now.

I wish I could say I laughed more then. I mostly cried. I wanted to be a mother so badly. I remember sitting in my car in a restaurant parking lot trying to muster the courage to go into a baby shower for a friend. I truly wanted to be happy for her, but I was so deep in the darkness of wanting to be pregnant myself, I just could not go in. So instead I prayed. I tried to bargain with God, I pleaded with him to make me a mother. I told him we would gladly accept any child, healthy or special needs. We just wanted to be parents, to be a family. Eventually, I became pregnant with BethAnne, Peyton, Walker, and surprise—Matthew!

I remember thinking during Matthew's infancy, how blessed we were. Four healthy children. I remembered the days of thinking I might never have a child, let alone four children. I was, and am, so grateful. When Matthew was initially diagnosed, Brett and I both struggled. We had so many questions: how could we fix this, how would autism affect our family, short-term and long-term, and so on. Later, we learned Matthew was also epileptic and experiencing absence seizures. More fears surfaced. Yet through it all, God was so faithful. He put the right people in our path: doctors, therapists, caregivers, family, friends, teachers, and Matthew has come so far.

One day, several years ago, in a very introspective moment, I realized that Matthew (as well as my other children) was an answer to a specific prayer. I truly believe that he came later in the progression, because I just was not ready for him yet. God had lots of work to do on me, on us, before we were prepared to parent Matthew. We do not get to choose our children; they are loaned to us for a time. Some of them longer than others. Our job is to love them, embrace them, teach them and then let them go, to the extent they can. My journey to Matthew prepared me to love and accept him just as he is, an answer to my prayers!

"Mrs. Mommy, Is Your Brain Tired?"

During one twelve-month period, Matthew's speech and language skills grew exponentially. It seemed that the language growth accompanied a decline in attention-seeking behaviors. He asked for specific food or drinks when he was hungry or thirsty. He sought help when he could not find something instead of tearing apart the room looking for it on his own. He let us know when he had had enough of a game or activity.

This is not to say that we do not still have plenty of room for improvement or days where we struggle, because we do, but we have to stop and appreciate the progress.

Some days the progress is less visible, if you are not looking for it. Matthew still uses a lot of movie talk in his communication. The improvement there is that he does not just repeat the scenes to himself anymore—now he wants to include someone else in his scenes. That someone has primarily been an immediate family member, his afterschool caregiver Mrs. Rhonda Robinson, or one of his therapists. Occasionally, he tries to get someone at school to join him, but they do not understand what he is asking of them.

He calls upon me to be a Wiggle or a Backyardigan or Charlie (he likes to be Lola). Sometimes I get to be Jesse, but mostly I am Woody to his Buzz Lightyear. There are days when he wants me to do a scene that I do not recognize, and he will repeat the lines to me over and over again. I cannot just repeat them—I have to say them in the right accent, with the right spacing and tone. If I fail to get it right, he models it for me and asks for me to do it again. I know he acquired these skills in the hours upon hours of speech therapy he worked through over the last ten years. He learned so much more than how to articulate his "r's" and his "l's".

Some days, I am preoccupied with life—worried about his siblings or what I am going to cook for dinner or how we are going to get him ready for the next hurdle— and I don't pay attention to his demands as closely as he likes. On one of those days, when he was asking lots of questions and I was not saying my part right, he suddenly said, "Mrs. Mommy, why are you not saying it right? Is your brain tired?"

I said, "Yes, Matthew, my brain is tired and I don't always know the answers."

He said, "Oh, but you do. You do know the answers."

Sweet Matthew, I love how much confidence you have in me. How I wish I knew all the answers, and I am so flattered that you think I do.

We moved on from that conversation, but his new expression, "Is your brain tired" stuck around. When I don't have a quick response or if I seem overwhelmed by his line of questioning, he asks, "Mrs. Mommy, is your brain tired?" Sometimes the answer is a simple yes, and other times it leads to a long explanation of why I don't know the answer or won't repeat what he wants me to.

Once, well maybe more than once, I have had to stop myself. I realize that I almost asked him to stop talking for a minute, something I told myself I would never do. You see, ten years ago when he did not talk and or ask questions, I told myself that if (and when) he finally talked I would never ask him to stop talking. During those days, my brain was tired from worrying about Matthew and trying to reach him, trying to figure out how to take care of his needs without neglecting his siblings, trying to hold it all together and "fix" things. This year on Good Friday, I was reminded that I can choose to be less tired, and I can rest in God's presence. Exodus 33:14 says, "...my presence shall go with thee and I will give thee rest." On this journey, I have learned that God is with me and my family and especially Matthew. He offers me his presence; I just have to be willing to rest in it.

"Let the little children come to me"

It was Easter Sunday, and I set aside time to write about a confluence of my Catholic faith and special needs children. In October of 2017, an Italian Special Olympics Team visited the Vatican as part of a recognition ceremony. Gemma, a five-year old girl with Down's Syndrome, was selected to present Pope Francis with a pair of red sneakers similar to those worn by the team. After presenting the Pope with the gift, Gemma hopped up into the Bishop's chair next to him. The girls' parents and the Pope's security immediately stepped forward to stop her, Francis waived them away and reached over to take her hand. He continued his remarks, saying, "You are a symbol of a sport that opens the eyes and heart to the value and dignity of individuals and people who otherwise would be the object of prejudice and exclusion."

Sometimes I struggle with Matthew and church; is he too loud or too wiggly, does he understand, will there be candles? (He doesn't like candles.) Pope Francis' words, and the picture of him speaking while holding young Gemma's hand, resonated with me and brought me to tears. I reached for my Bible searching for the scripture that filled my heart, Matthew 19:14: *"Let the little children come to me and do not hinder them, for the kingdom of heaven belongs to such as these."* Francis gave us such a poignant example of Jesus' directive in this moment and in all moments, he reminded me that Jesus invites ALL of us to come to him, just as we are, just where we are. In turn, we should invite all, of any ability, to join us in work, in play, and in worship.

Amazing Love

Our family is Catholic, and we attend mass weekly. Matthew attends an additional mass with his classmates at school, along with daily morning prayer. Over the years, his participation in the mass has grown, but he's never shown any interest in singing any of the prayers or hymns. It's ironic that he purposefully chooses not to sing in church because he loves to sing at home. He sings along with the Wiggles, he sings Disney songs, he sings the Cars song. Occasionally he hears a song on the radio that he likes, and he will ask to put it on his iPad and then he sings along with that too!

So last fall in church, you can imagine my surprise when Matthew began to sing along with the hymn *Amazing Love*:

Amazing love, how can it be?
  That You, my King would die for me?
  Amazing love, I know it's true
  It's my joy to honor You
  In all I do, I honor You[KT2] [5]

Brett, the other kids and I were shocked when Matthew sang along with the words on the projector screen in the front of the sanctuary. He had the sweetest smile on his face and sang loud enough for us to hear. We were all afraid to show our joy because we were afraid he would stop singing. I thought he knew the song from school services and was comfortable singing it because of that. However, when I asked at school, they said that he does not sing along there. I guess on that particular Saturday evening the conditions in church and Matthew's mindset aligned, and he was moved to sing. It was a beautiful moment, and I was filled with amazing love for my little family and for my God.

Matthew has not sung along with a hymn since then, but he recently started singing the Alleluias in church. I'm hoping that he continues to grow in his participation at his own pace, just like he does with most other things in life.

Get Jesus

Matthew's fear of fire intensified over the past year. He jumps at the mention of the word and replies, "Don't say fire." He blows out candles when I light them in the house. He shrinks in fear of the candles at church. He could not bring himself to participate in the blessing of the throats, despite the blessing using unlit candles or Stations of the Cross during Lent. His last question before he gets out of the car at school in the morning is, "Will there be a fire drill today?" I really think the fear of fire comes out of his fear of the sudden, loud sounds associated with fire—drills, alarms and sirens—but he has not confirmed that for me.

Considering these fears and the deviation from routine, I began to prepare him for Ash Wednesday services. He would attend a mass and ashes service at Sacred Heart Cathedral School with his peers. I knew he would associate the ashes with fire and be afraid. On the Tuesday evening before Ash Wednesday, I again explained the process to him: the priest would make the sign of a cross of his forehead with ashes, cold ashes, while saying, "Remember, you are dust, and to dust you shall return." The explanation seemed to put his mind at ease and he went about his evening.

The next day while waiting in car line I asked his teacher how the service went. She explained that she too had prepared him for the process and he seemed ok with it. However, when they reached the front of the line, he just couldn't do it. So, he told the Bishop, "No thank you, I will just have Jesus," and continued back to his seat and waited patiently for communion. He participated in the Holy Eucharist, like he always does and was happy to "get Jesus." While I was disappointed that he could not get comfortable enough to participate, I was relieved that he was polite, and I was amazed by his explanation.

Years ago, as we prepared Matthew to participate in Catholic sacraments, we struggled with how to explain our belief in the Holy Eucharist. It's difficult for an adult to comprehend the Catechism of the Catholic Church, consecration and transubstantiation, let alone a seven-year-old with autism. After counseling with our priest, Father Michael Nixon, we decided to explain to Matthew that when we take communion we "take Jesus" and we prepare for that throughout the course of each Mass. Matthew converted "take Jesus" to "get Jesus" and has fully participated in the sacraments since his First Reconciliation and First Communion. There have been times when I wondered about his understanding of it all, but his response to the Bishop on Ash Wednesday provided me with some comfort or assurance that he does understand. He knew he wanted to "get Jesus" at Mass. Is that not what most Christian believers, regardless of denomination, hope to take away from their weekly services? Don't we all want to "get" Jesus? I know I do.

What's a Funeral?

In Matthew's lifetime, he's been fortunate to only experience death in terms of pets and not people. I don't intend to diminish the loss of a pet; they are family members, and their loss is painful to all of us. But Matthew is fortunate in that he has not lost a grandparent or aunt or uncle, no close family friends. He has seen death in movies, and we have discussed it in simple terms.

Earlier this school year, a student at Matthew's school tragically died over a weekend. The loss devastated the entire school family. I knew I needed to prepare Matthew for the atmosphere he would face at school on Monday. Contrary to the belief that people with autism do not show empathy, Matthew can be very empathetic. If he notices someone sad or crying, he tries to provide comfort. I explained to him as simply as I could that something very sad had occurred to one of the students and that his classmates and teachers might be sad and emotional at school. He listened and did not say anything further.

His teacher and I texted over the weekend to make sure we were on the same page with what he knew and how we thought he might react. I made sure she knew that when he experiences sadness, he usually relates it back to other sad occurrences in his life, like the loss of our pets. He will list each of them individually and talk about their deaths.

On Monday, I received a phone call saying that he was sad and asking if it was okay for him to speak with one of the grief counselors. I consented and shared what I had shared with his teacher about how he reacts to sadness. After school, he told me that he was sad at school. His friends were sad. "Some people cried and that made me sad." I told him that it was ok, that sometimes expressing our sadness makes us feel better. He did not want to talk about it anymore and went about his afternoon.

Brett and I had already decided that Matthew would not attend the funeral. I was not sure how he would react and did not want any of the teachers or staff to be distracted from their own grief and supporting the students grieving the loss of their friend. I picked him up before the funeral and we spent quality time together.

The next morning on the way to school, in the midst of normal morning conversation, he asked, "Mom, what's a funeral?" I felt a lump in my throat. I suddenly realized just how much of the surrounding conversation he absorbed the last few days at school. I told him, "A funeral is the celebration of the life of someone who has died and the ceremony is usually held in a church or community center." I went on, "There was a funeral yesterday at church for the student who died." He was quiet for a minute and said, "Ok, mom." That was it, no more conversation on the topic. It resonated with me:

he hears everything, he processes it and then talks about it in his own time and own way.

[5] Foote, Billy James. Phillips, Craig, and Dean "Amazing Love." Let My Words Be Few, Sparrow Records, 2001, Track 6, www.lyrics.com/-lyric/14814030/51MustHaveWorshipClassics/YouAreMyKingAmazin-gLove

8

Teachable Moments

Words Hurt

The Merriam Webster dictionary defines retarded as "slow or limited in intellectual or emotional development."

There was a time when I was guilty of using the "R" word, retarded, in the course of normal conversation. I referred to myself or ideas as "retarded." I did not stop to think about who I might be hurting or how offensive it might be to others; that all changed the day Matthew met the criteria to be labeled "intellectually disabled."

In that moment, I realized how insensitive I was all those times I casually tossed the "R" word around. I was overcome with guilt. I vowed to myself that I would not use the word inappropriately again. However, I was a coward when it came to informing others about how much the use of the word hurt me. I feared the tears that might come if I tried to explain to a friend or family member or perfect stranger, how their inappropriate use of a word cuts me to the core. I feared how my children's friends might react if I corrected them on their word choice or what they might relay to their parents about crazy Mrs. Parra. I changed my own word usage and talked with my other children about making sure they did not use "the word," but I didn't try to change anyone else.

Then in 2010 I read about a Milton teenager, Katie Smith, who started a campaign at Milton High School to end the use of the "R" word amongst her peers. Katie's older brother is intellectually disabled and she decided to try to educate her peers and advocate for change. I was deeply moved, but still I was silent.

Since that time, BethAnne, Peyton and Walker have come home on occasion from school or other activities offended by someone's inappropriate or offensive use of the "R" word. This unintended slight is not limited to children or teens; the words often come from the mouths of adults. No matter the source, the words hurt. Often, they are just empty words to the person saying them, but they are tied to a loved one for the listener.

At our home, we use these days as teachable moments (there are lots of teachable moments for siblings of a special needs person). We discuss how those moments make us feel, what we could have or should have said or done, and how we can learn from the moment. We also discussed how over the past nine years we learned Matthew's intelligence or emotional growth might be different that the norm, it is definitely not less!

Every time I have sat down to write, I have struggled with writing about this topic. It's touchy, I know, but I needed to write about it. I needed to own my failures, to apologize to anyone I ever offended when I chose the wrong word. And not just the "R" word, but other words that are offensive to a race, or religion, or gender, or ethnicity. Now, I am learning. I still stumble, but I try to choose my words more thoughtfully, and I challenge you to do the same. You never know whose sibling or mom or dad or friend you might be speaking to, and you might not know that they walk away with a heavy heart.

"Fidiot"

I'm clearly not a fan of the "R" word and am very sensitive to the use of its synonyms: moron, idiot, stupid, etc. We made a very conscious effort, even before Matthew's diagnosis, not to use those words inappropriately in our conversations around our children. Once Matthew received a diagnosis, began receiving therapy, and ultimately began to speak, we made an even greater effort to eliminate these words from conversation. Since Matthew mimicked much of what he heard, we did not want him to use bad language or hurtful words. We went to such lengths that Matthew, even now, corrects anyone he hears using one of those words and makes me change them to "nicer" words when we find them in a book. Thankfully, not the "R" word, he has either not heard it or does not associate it with the other "bad" words. He has never used it in front of me.

Sometimes, he hears these words in movies. Our beloved Pixar movies are notorious for using them. Matthew will remind me that in *Toy Story 2*, Ham calls someone a "moron". He says, "Pixar can say 'moron', but Matthew can't."

I agree; Matthew can't.

This past year he discovered a new word, "fidiot." I cannot put a definite date on when he started using it. I do remember him saying, "Matthew can't say idiot, but he can say fidiot." I know that I could not clearly understand him; the word was kind of muffled. I told him we should not call anyone names of any kind and moved on. For several weeks, he asked about his new word, off and on. Obviously, I did not really hear him or ponder what this word might mean. Anyone who knows me well knows that I have little tolerance for cursing and little tolerance for the "F" word (no, not fat). So, it never occurred to me that my sweet Matthew would, even unintentionally, find a way to work that word into his vocabulary.

One day I experienced a light bulb moment watching a movie when someone said "F....... idiot." I flashed back to a time he was scripting "Matthew can't say idiot, but he can say fidiot," I realized with horror where "fidiot" must have come from. My innocent Matthew for weeks had been saying f..... idiot. What? How could he have learned this? Who said this in front of him? My mind searched for answers and I ultimately concluded that one of the YouTube channels he watches must include close captioning with f..... idiot and because he didn't know what the f stood for, thank God, he just combined it into a new word—fidiot. I knew this habit must be changed quickly and in such a way that he did not grasp on to it tightly and refuse to let go. If he knows something really pushes your buttons, he files it away and uses it at just the right (or wrong) moment. My friends who know how I feel about cursing have enjoyed quite a few laughs with me over this one. Fortunately, "fidiot" disappeared from Matthew's vocabulary almost as quickly as it appeared, and no colorful words replaced it. I assure you, every time I hear someone use that phrase, the same thoughts come to mind, "I really wish they wouldn't say that," and "if they must, can't they use Matthew's more subtle version."

"The Idiot Guide"

One Easter weekend we went to Houma to visit Brett's parents. On Thursday night Matthew and I had some alone time in the hotel while Brett and Walker visited with family. We were piled up in the bed watching a movie when Matthew announced, "I can't say 'idiot'!"

I replied with my standard, "It's not a nice word!"

He pushed, "Why can't I say idiot? The books say it."

I asked, "What books?"

"The books that say *The Idiot Guide* on the front" he explained.

I thought to myself, "He's got me." I thought I would probe further, "Where did you see those books with the bad word on the front?"

"The library," he stated. "Why do they say the bad word?" he asked innocently.

I did not then and still do not have a good answer for him. In the moment I said, "Matthew, I just do not know."

He asked what he always does when I say, "I don't know", "Is your brain tired?"

"No Matthew my brain is not tired, I just do not know the answer." He moved on, but I have not. That exchange has weighed heavily on my mind since then. Why did the author/founder of that book series HAVE to use that word in the book title?

According to Webster's dictionary idiot means, "a foolish or stupid person." I was intrigued to learn the origin of the word idiot. The clinical origin of the word was to describe someone whose mental development did not exceed that of a two-year-old. Is that the target audience of this book series or its relative the "Dummies"? One of the founders when prompted about the title responded that the word "Dummy" was a term of endearment. I do not think so.

Maybe the founders and authors of these books did not intend to insult anyone with the title, and maybe I am one of the few who is insulted. I did not come to this place of understanding on my own. Matthew led me here. He keeps me honest. He remembers the rules and while he does not always follow them (right Mrs. L and Mrs. Susann?), he notices when others do not follow them as well. We, and I mean that in the most collective way possible, must watch what we say and do and write because Matthew is watching, taking notes and will remind us when we break the rules!

9

Advocating Like a Mother!

To the Family of the Newly Diagnosed

Dear Friends,

I can call you that, right?

Almost 10 years ago exactly Matthew received his Autism Spectrum Diagnosis; some days it seems like a lifetime ago, and others like yesterday. I remember sitting in three different doctor's offices in a 10-day window, and all three concluded, "pervasive developmental disorder-not otherwise specified"in other words, Autism Spectrum Disorder.

Looking back, it felt like I was on the outside looking in, watching a movie of my life I hoped the doctors would have a surprise diagnosis that was easily treated. The moment those words registered in my mind, I cried, and then I experienced overwhelming and unexpected sense of relief. Now we could access services, we could develop a treatment plan, we could educate ourselves and our family on how to help Matthew grow into the best version of himself, and we could stop wondering what we were facing.

Right now, you might be reeling, but the ship will steady. The rough seas will be interrupted by periods of calm, but you never completely relax. You likely feel alone at times, but you are not. You may be afraid of what lies ahead, of making the wrong decisions, of how autism will change your life. I will not lie and say that it will be easy. It is not easy, but parenting never is. Cut yourself some slack, and take the time to process that while your child might not follow the path you previously planned for them, that can happen with any child, not just autistic ones.

Read that last part again, "that can happen with any child, not just autistic ones."

Things happen in life that change the path of a child: disease, accidents, poor choices. We adjust the plans.

Lean on your spouse or your partner. You each may approach autism differently. You will have different fears or concerns. You will have different strengths when working with your child or young adult. Any challenge that arises with children, not just autism, can be hard on relationships and marriage. Do not let those challenges overshadow your shared your love for your child and your desire to see him become the best version of himself. Work together!

When you are ready, assemble a team. A team that includes doctors, therapists, teachers, family members, caregivers, other parents of older, autistic children or adults. and friends. All of them play vital roles. Listen to them, do your homework, and make informed. educated decisions. Listen closely to the voices in your head and in your heart. Sometimes you will agree with the professionals, and sometimes you will not. Make sure that when you disagree with them, that you have a basis for your dissent, and it is not because you are in denial. You will experience both.

Some people will stay on your team, while others will walk away. You will laugh and cry with your team, and if you pray, you will pray with and for your team.

Find a parent or some parents of children slightly older than yours and pick their brains. Even though we all know that every autistic person is different, there are lessons to be learned from those who have gone before you. Ask them for recommendations, ask them what they would do differently, ask them what they would repeat. They know the road you are walking. They will likely be happy to help. They will become your friends.

While you make new friends in the autistic community, try to maintain your old friendships. Some of your old friends will disappoint you, probably not because they do not care, but because they do not know how to help or are afraid of saying the wrong thing. It is okay, because other friends will surprise you; they will not just stick around, they will step into your new normal and advocate for your child. They will teach their children how to accept your child, they will invite you and your child into their homes, and they will lift you up.

If you have other children, know that while they may struggle at times, their lives will be enriched by their sibling with autism. They will learn that life is not fair. They will learn valuable lessons about hard work. They will learn to advocate for others. They will learn to find joy in little things. They will be the teacher at times and the student at others. They will play with toys they have outgrown and watch movies they do not like. They will love fiercely.

Presume competence in your child. Think about what you say in front of and in hearing distance of your child. You may think that he does not understand you, but do not risk it. We have learned that Matthew understands and takes in far more than he immediately communicates back to us. We also learned that just because he is not looking does not mean he is not listening. As his communication skills have improved and grown more sophisticated, he verbalized things he remembered from years past. So far, it has not been anything I was ashamed of saying or doing.

Progress may be slow, and your child may experience periods of plateau or regression. Never give up. Take a step back and a deep breath and go to Plan B. Plan B could involve a new school, new medications, new therapists—just not all at the same time. Always have a Plan B. Help your child to overcome his or her challenges, and look for opportunities to improve his strengths. Your child will change you and challenge you in ways you cannot imagine.

You may do things you said you "never" would. I pray that when you have been on this road as long as I have, you will be grateful for the lessons learned, the experiences shared and the unconditional love you now know how to give and receive. Hopefully, you will take the chance to reach out to others who are new to the journey and give them a hand up.

Sincerely,

Mrs. Mommy

Sometimes if I listen close enough, I hear voices...

You know that little voice in your head that speaks to you when you are still and silent or when you are about to make a big mistake. Depending on your beliefs or your faith, you may believe it is your conscience or you may think it is God. More times than not, I think it is God trying to get my attention, to give me direction, to send me the signs I am constantly praying or asking for.

Over the summer, I began to hear that voice in my head regarding one of Matthew's regular afternoon activities. I was not sure we were seeing progress or benefit from the time and money we were investing in it. I began to wish we had that time to allow him to explore other interests. As the same time as the appearance of that little voice in my head (or heart), Matthew began to ask not to go. He came up with lots of reasons, like he was tired or did not feel well or just did not want to go, but I questioned our motivations for "quitting." We persisted in our attendance, but the little voice continued.

Summer was in full swing at this point, and Matthew spent every available moment he could in our backyard pool. He jumped off of our waterfall platform about a hundred times a day. He splashed his hands-on top of the water and watched the drops ricochet into different directions. He put on his merman fin (yes, thanks to BethAnne, we have a merman fin) and his swim cap and sat on the steps as long as I would let him. There must have been some amazing sensory input from the fin and cap because he began to ask to wear them outside of the pool, in the bath tub, in the office while he played on the computer, and on long car trips. Eventually he learned he could kick in the pool with that fin and he began to swim with it, in between sitting spells on the steps. And still the voice in my head, if we cancel X activity, we can explore something new.

As summer drew to a close and fall approached, I knew our pool water temperature would fall and Matthew would no longer be comfortable swimming in it. His time in the water brought him so much joy that I began to consider other options for getting him in the water. I asked Matthew what he thought about taking a break from our other activity and trying something new, something like swim lessons. He immediately asked if he could wear a fin and a cap. I explained that he could definitely wear a cap, but for swim lessons, you wear two fins, not a merman one. I heeded the little voice in my head with Matthew's encouragement and put our activity on hold for a month. My next call was to my friend, Robin Heller, who coincidentally, is the Seastars Aquatics Head Swim Coach.

For quite some time, Robin had been encouraging me to bring Matthew to Seastars. Seastars is a local swim team that reaches "children who are economically, physically, and mentally challenged by providing individualized attention as a part of a structured competitive swim team program." I made lots of excuses for why we could not: the time, homework, the drive, conflicts with the Greater Pensacola Aquatic Club (GPAC) commitments that Walker is a part of, Matthew was not ready, and so on… Robin, in her infinite wisdom, convinced me that Seastars would meet Matthew where he was, and so we made a plan to begin.

I would be lying if I said the first few lessons (or weeks of lessons) were easy. Matthew worked so hard, but had a hard time getting his arms and legs to work at the same time, getting comfortable with wearing goggles and putting his face in the water, learning how to breathe without getting water in his nose, and so on. He talked a lot during practice and asked a million times, "What's next?" I am certain it drove Coach Gracie crazy. It was hard for me to watch, wanting to help him so much, but knowing he had to learn and that I had to let Robin and Gracie develop a rapport with him. Slowly but surely, he began to progress, and his confidence began to grow. The real turning point came during a series of private lessons with Robin. She truly has a gift with children. She has just the right amount of toughness, motivation and love to get the kids to believe they can do anything. She gets in the water on their level and she meets them where they are. I am so grateful to her.

Now, about six months later, you can see, and almost feel, the excitement in his face when he masters a new piece of a stroke or is able to coordinate his stroke and his kick. He recently began to work on butterfly arms and was so proud when he got both arms out of the water together the first time. He looked up at Robin and yelled, "I did it!" He wakes up every Monday and Wednesday excited about going to Seastars after school. He takes pride in wearing his Seastars shirt. He knows he is working hard and getting better. He wants me to video him swimming and he watches it back, over and over again. One thing has not changed: he still loves to wear fins, of the merman or swimmer variety. Sometimes on really good days or really tough ones, he wears them in the bathtub. One day I hope he can fully explain to me what they do for him. Until then, I will continue to listen to Matthew and that little voice in my head when making decisions about what to do and what not to do and, in the words of Dory, I will encourage him to "just keep swimming."

"Just Keep Swimming..."

As I have mentioned, SEASTARS Aquatics is a one-of-a-kind swim team, (literally, one-of-a-kind) for low-income or special needs swimmers in a training environment. If you qualify, swim team is a free program funded by private lesson revenue, grants and public support. You can't really begin to appreciate SEASTARS from afar you have to be a part of it, you have to watch it, you have to hear it, you have to feel it. It is like nothing I have been a part of before.

Coach Robin, the head coach and one of the founders, and her coaching staff are real-life miracle workers. They take children who literally will not even get in the water and transform them into competitive swimmers. They continue to amaze me with their work on, and off, the pool deck, and I am so grateful for the role they play in Matthew's life.

A few years ago, we would have been happy for Matthew simply to be swimming regularly, a lesson and a practice a week. The main objective was to have him exercise and for him to be safe in and around the water.

As his skills developed under Coach Robin, our expectations grew a bit. Perhaps he would swim some summer league meets or Special Olympics, eventually once he was legal in his strokes he might even swim a USA Swimming Meet, just like his older siblings, or as he says, "like Walker." Robin pulls out all the stops when working with her swimmers. She meets them where they are, she's creative, she finds their motivation. One of the drills Matthew loves is to swim with a traffic cone tied to his waist with fins on. He loves the sensory feedback that drill provides. I love how creative Robin is in her teaching techniques. Somehow, she treats every swimmer on the team equally and fairly while meeting them where they are with just what they need to be successful, which is about 57 different places. Success does not mean winning in the traditional sense here, it means "winning" in the best sense: winning at SEASTARS Aquatics means becoming a better version of oneself.

I always preach about presuming competence to teachers, to my family, to anyone who will listen; "we should presume competence in our kids until they prove otherwise." If I'm honest I have not always followed this mantra with Matthew and swimming. I was reluctant for him to participate in a USA Swimming meet, because I was afraid of failure, afraid he would not be able to do it, afraid I would cry, just afraid. Robin insisted we sign up for a meet in January, "Just the 50 free" she said. "It's the first event on Friday. He can do this!"

Reluctantly I signed him up and she worked tirelessly with him to get him ready. Coach Robin ensured his accommodations were in place. He could start from the water, she could prompt his start with a touch, he could be in an outside lane. All the pieces were in place for success, but I was still worried. When the day came, I was nervous for him (and me). Coach Robin took him to the blocks and I found my spot to watch. I asked a friend to videotape because I knew my hands would not be steady. My eyes welled with tears as I watched Walker's GPAC family and Matthew's SEASTARS family line up on both ends of the pool to cheer him on. He did it; he raced the 50 freestyle legally in a USA Swimming meet. There were lots of tears from me and our family friends and there was immense pride from all of our swimming family and there was a little guilt in my heart for not encouraging him to try it sooner.

The next week at practice, he received a ribbon for a best time. He was so proud standing on that pool deck, smiling for the camera; that was all the affirmation I needed to continue encouraging him to swim. Fast forward to March, and he swam in his second meet, 50 freestyle. Coach Robin prepared him to swim faster, to try to swim a best time, she practiced "racing" with him and guess what? He swam a best time by 10 seconds, and again there were tears and pride. He says, "I'm swimming like Walker." Yes, Matthew, you are.

I attended when SEASTARS hosted its first swim banquet in its thirteen-year history. I wish you could have been there to celebrate with us. I wish every donor or sponsor or grantor that ever gave even a dollar to the program could have peeked in the window to see their impact of their donations. Their contributions are changing lives every single day. The banquet was a beautiful melding of swimmers, families, and coaches celebrating the amazing achievements of swimmers doing things that many of their parents never dreamed they would accomplish. Young swimmers next to older ones, non-verbal children sitting with those who never stop talking, swimmers from different backgrounds, races, and abilities celebrating their accomplishments together over tacos and cake. Seastars' swimmers do not just learn how to swim; they learn valuable life lessons about setting goals, working hard, sharing and maintaining a positive attitude through it all. We recognized athletic success, community service, sportsmanship, perseverance, leadership and attendance. We laughed and we cried. We shared a meal, like a family. We came together to celebrate SEASTARS and all it stands for, which is so much more than swimming.

What I Want People to Know About Matthew-Part 2

When Matthew and I are out at Target, the grocery store, swim meets, or the flag pole at school, children who do not know him (and even some who do) stare when he sings or dances or acts out a script with me or wears headphones outside. I read their little faces, full of wonder, confusion, and even fear. I see them turn to their moms, dads, grandparents or sitters and whisper, "What's wrong with him?" or, "Why is he doing that?" These children are not mean or bullies, they are just children and they are curious. I want to speak up and explain. I want to teach them about Matthew and autism, but most of the time I do not. I do not want to overstep. I secretly hope they will ask me, instead of their parents, because I am longing to tell them about autism, about Matthew.

So here is what I want your children to know about Matthew: He's an eleven-year-old boy who also happens to be autistic. It is autism; it is not chicken pox, or the plague. It is not contagious or terminal (and I thank God for that every day). It is a disorder that affects how his brain works. I do not believe there is a cure for autism. There are therapies that help autistics overcome their challenges, but the challenges do not go away. Some parents choose not to talk about their children's diagnosis; they do not want to label them. However, I feel like explaining autism (and how it affects Matthew) can make his behaviors easier to understand. If he were diabetic, or blind, or dyslexic, or anything else, I would feel the same way. I do not ever want him to be ashamed of being autistic; it is part of who he is. Autism shapes his challenges and his gifts!

As with any disorder or disability, some things come easier than others. For example, some of the medications he takes affect his ability to write and play ball. Just because he does not speak like a typical eleven-year-old boy does not mean that he does not enjoy some of the same things typical eleven-year-old boys do. Like most eleven-year old's, he likes swimming, eating at McDonald's, building with Legos (mostly things that do not come in a kit), playing outside, and shooting hoops. He is a little shy; his brain processes things differently than most brains, and it takes him a little longer to answer a question. So, if you ask him a question, give him time to answer. If you keep repeating the question or move on to another question, you will just confuse him. He wears headphones to lunch and assemblies because the loud environment can be too overwhelming for him without them. I could go on and on. If you have a question I did not address, please ask or let your children ask.

If you want to be his friend, you might have to invest a little time in him. Learn what he likes to do or watch or talk about, and engage in that activity. Once you gain his trust, he might try playing a game you like or watching your favorite movie. He has some hidden talents, like saying his ABCs backwards; he once did that for a talent show at school. He has great balance and little fear. He wants to have friends and be a friend. If you do not know what to do, just ask. Ask me, ask a teacher, but just ask. Remember, that he is different, but not less.

Before I knew it Matthew was thirteen. The older (and larger) he gets, the more difficult it is for him to blend in. Adults stare in wonder at the grocery store as he asks me questions repeatedly, as we repeat his favorite script for the tenth time in ten minutes, or as we sing The Wiggles at the top of our lungs. Sometimes I will volunteer that he is autistic and this is what we do to get through the stress of the grocery store, but then they look at me with pity in their eyes. I do not want their pity, just their acceptance of Matthew.

Young children do not just stare—they ask questions and that is why they are my favorite. Still, I love for people to ask questions about Matthew, because that opens the door for me to tell them everything I want them to know or everything they need to know. Their parents will try to stop them, but I encourage them to continue. It gives me an opportunity to educate them about autism.

Middle school kids are either the best or a challenge or somewhere in between. The best, school friends like Caroline, Mary, and Willie, are constant friends and defenders. Then there are the lifelong friends (you know who you are) who make time for Matthew anytime, anywhere. These friends, new and old, look out for him. They don't need an explanation; they are just his friends. They are the hands and feet of Jesus in the way they care for Matthew. The challenges are the more silent ones. They just stare and then look away, and never ask questions.

The ones in the middle want to be his friend—you can see it in their eyes—but they just do not know what to do. They are not mean; they just are not inclusive either.

I do not know if they are afraid or embarrassed. I want to tell them that autism is not contagious; they will not catch it by being his friend. I want to tell them that Matthew would love to be their friend; he just does not always know where to begin. He might not know how to play the games they enjoy or he might not have seen the movie they just saw. I want to explain that he uses "movie talk" to communicate emotions that he does not have the words to explain. I want to tell them to slow down when they do speak to him because his brain does not process their words or questions as quickly as other kids might. Sometimes he will answer a question several minutes or even an hour after I've asked him. It is just how his mind works. I would tell them that while he may never remember their name, he has an amazing memory for other tiny details, like what kind of charm they have on their backpack or what kind of sticker is on their laptop case, or in what scene of the CoCo movie the Buzz Lightyear piñata is hidden.

I would tell them that he picks his nose and his fingernails when he is anxious, and he does not understand that is not "socially acceptable" behavior in middle school, but it is a coping mechanism for him. I would tell them that he is very sensitive, that he loves deeply, that his feelings do get hurt and that he has great remorse when he hurts someone else. I would tell them that he wants to have friends, and he wants to be a friend; he just cannot always overcome the challenges necessary to be friends in the traditional middle-school world. He might need them to be brave like Caroline, Mary and Willie, and take a step into his world: draw on childhood memories of television shows or Disney movies they enjoyed when they were younger and talk with Matthew. They might be surprised—both the other children and Matthew—about what they have in common. I would say if you do not know what to do around Matthew, just ask. Ask me, ask a teacher, but do not be afraid to ask. Most important is to remember that he is different, but not less, and treat him how you would want to be treated.

Don't Be Afraid to Ask

On a recent visit to my brother and sister-in-law's house in Texas, my nephews asked lots of great questions about Matthew. They wanted to know why he did certain things. "Why is he calm in the morning and not so calm in the evening? Why does he like to wear headphones? Why won't he let me watch on the iPad with him?" Beautiful, appropriate questions that I was so happy to answer.

Guess what? I wish more children asked me questions, children in the grocery store or on the playground and especially children that attend school with Matthew. Answering their questions gives me an opportunity to advocate for Matthew and enlighten others about autism. I can explain why he does what he does. He repeats Movie Talk when he cannot find his own words; he wears headphones when the sounds are too loud or too sudden for him; he is calm in the morning after a good night's rest, fresh medications and a plan for the day and not so calm in the evening because he has coped with challenges all day and his medications are wearing off; he does not like to share his iPad, the way you do not want to share your blanket, it makes him comfortable That is all it took. Simple questions, simple answers, more acceptance.

I will go one step further; I wish more adults felt secure asking questions when they do not understand. Or that parents would not shush their kids out of embarrassment when they ask questions. I challenge and encourage you to ask me or any other special needs parent respectful questions about our children. While I cannot speak for everyone, I think most of us are happy to try to explain. We want you to feel comfortable interacting with our children; we want you to understand as best you can how to engage with them and, most importantly, we want them to feel welcome and safe as they venture into "the world."

We all have our idiosyncrasies: we do not like tags in our clothes, we do not like certain textures under our bare feet, we do not like our foods to touch, we cannot stand certain pitches of sound. We just cope with our challenges differently. For Matthew, the coping can get overwhelming and lead to non-preferred behaviors. When people understand the warning signs that accompany this increasing difficulty to cope, they judge less and accept more. For this reason, we chose a more open approach to speaking about Matthew's autism. While we fully respect Matthew's privacy, and I ask for his permission to write about his journey, we also acknowledge that he is autistic, just like he has brown eyes and brown hair.

Helicopter Mom

According to Dr. Haim Ginott's 1969 parenting book, a "helicopter parent" is one who "hovers" over their teenager like a helicopter. The Urban Dictionary defines a helicopter mom as one "who is overly involved in the life of their child. They tend to hover over their every movement and decision."

Hello, my name is Rocky, and I am a helicopter mom. I know, the truth hurts sometimes, but this is a truth I can own. Here is the deal: I have been a helicopter mom for almost 21 years. When I finally became a mom after years of struggling with infertility, I was a little over protective of my first child. I drove the grandmothers crazy. I did not want to share BethAnne with anyone, including them. I was afraid something would happen to her, that she would get sick or not eat enough or not develop properly if we did not do everything just so.

My willingness to share soon changed.

We got the surprise of our lives when we learned I was pregnant with Peyton when BethAnne was five months old. I was tired and morning sick and overwhelmed by the idea of having two babies. I became a little more laid back—just a little, though. I wanted to make sure the girls were getting exposed to all the right things and none of the wrong ones. I hovered all the time.

Walker arrived a few years later. I was a few years older and a little more laid back. I learned which battles to fight and what to let slide, at least in the toddler world. I still wanted the best for my kids, but I learned that some things would not be perfect, and we could not do everything all the time. We would not all be bilingual or musical prodigies or athletic phenoms, but we could be humble and kind. We could leave the world a better place than we found it and we could cultivate our God-given gifts. What worked for one child might not work for another; unfortunately, it was trial by fire.

Fast forward a few more years, and Matthew arrived. Our surprise fourth child. When Matthew was born, I was fully immersed in my role as "helicopter" mom; parenting four kids under eight was no small feat. We spent a lot of time in the car, going to school, to piano lessons, to swim team, to soccer, and so on. The big kids were all at one school, Matthew was at another. I volunteered and played tennis in between hovering opportunities.

When Matthew was around 18 months old, we determined Matthew was regressing developmentally. His language was disappearing, his eye contact was gone, and we thought he might be deaf. Providers assured us they believed he was just the typical last child, late developing, everyone-does-everything-for-him boy, and he was not autistic. He just needed some speech therapy, maybe some occupational therapy as well. He would catch up.

As Matthew continued to regress and we sought answers, I honed my hovering skills. I hovered at school, at home, at church, at therapy. I wanted to ensure that I could document every new word, every changed behavior, every meltdown. I wanted to make sure I knew all the questions to ask each new specialist. Ultimately, some brave doctor finally made the call and diagnosed Matthew with PDD-NOS (pervasive development disorder-not otherwise specified, also known as Autism). Before that day, I was an amateur helicopter mom; soon I would become a professional. If we are honest here, I think most parents of special needs children own the helicopter label.

I am, by necessity, overly involved in every aspect of Matthew's life. I do hover over his movement and decisions. I linger when we are in unfamiliar places, when we meet new people, and when I am afraid that he is having a bad day. I brood over decisions about where to go to school, what medications to allow, what summer activities he should do. I fret, I stress, I hover because I am afraid. I think that is what drives most of us helicopter moms—fear! Fear that we are going mess up our child's life. God shares this precious child with us, and we cannot screw it up!

Most of the time I believe the hovering helps. We work as translators or tour guides, though sometimes when we overstep, we can be a detriment and limit independence when we do not presume competence. It is a fine line.

In the essence of full disclosure, I still hover over my neuro-typical children too. I worry about where they are and who they are with. Are they getting enough sleep? Eating their veggies? Using their manners? My attention is spread a little thin, but I find a way. BethAnne, Peyton and Walker will confirm that I can hover with the best of them, though I pray they know it is because I only want them to be the best version of themselves!

So again, let me introduce myself. My name is Rocky, and I'm a helicopter mom.

Imposter Syndrome

Do you ever stop and wonder, "How did I get here?" or, "Who are these children, and am I really responsible for them?" or, "Do they know I really don't have the experience or knowledge to do this job?" Furthermore, did you know there's actually a name for this? It's called Imposter Syndrome.

I listen to a Catholic radio showed hosted by Jennifer Fulwiler on a fairly regular basis while waiting in the carline[6]. She is a former atheist, and a mother of six who has written two books and has an interesting array of guests each week. One of her recent guests talked about experiencing "imposter syndrome," I was unfamiliar with the term and was intrigued—so during the commercial break I googled the phrase.

The term, which dates back to 1978, "describes a feeling of phoniness in people who believe that they are not intelligent, capable or creative despite evidence of high achievement." [7] The guest used the term, not in reference to high achievement, but more in terms of finding ourselves in situations for which we feel unprepared or unqualified, but amazingly outsiders seem to think we are qualified and have our act together. As I read the definition, I made a note to explore the topic further at a later date.

So here I am, thinking. I am going to theorize that a lot of us experience those days where we just cannot fathom how we got where we are: work-wise, parenting-wise, in our volunteerism, etc... People put their trust and faith to use to get jobs done, money raised, and so on. God loans our precious children to us, and we try to raise them as best we can. Yet, I am going to take this a step further with parents of special needs children. I think we probably feel like imposters fairly regularly, like we are not sure we are equipped to raise this child or these children, like we do not know how to do this.

Don't get me wrong—we know our kids really well, and we want what is best for them. We want them to have access to everything typical children do, that is also appropriate for them. But every time I sit in an IEP meeting or visit a specialist or share our story with others, I feel a bit like an imposter. It might appear as if I have my act together, and know what I am doing, but really deep inside, I'm kinda like, "Holy cow! How did I get here? I hope they don't figure out how little I know and how much of my plan is just putting one foot in front of the other, taking one day at a time. Maybe they won't see through the facade." Any other special needs parents feel that way? I'm guessing there are a few heads nodding out there.

Dear Teenagers

Dear Teenagers,

Some of you really get Matthew. You know him, you accept him, and you meet him right where he is. You will never know how eternally grateful I am for your kindness and your acceptance. I see your kindness, and sometimes I try to express my appreciation, but it makes me emotional and that makes you uncomfortable. So, I try to just say "thank you," even though I never feel like a simple thank you is enough!

Some of you do not really get Matthew, do not accept him, do not meet him where he is. I do not know if it comes from fear or lack of understanding. I see you, too. I see the looks exchanged with friends, the eye rolls, the unwillingness to accept. It breaks my heart. Here is what I want you to know about Matthew and other kids who are different.

I know Matthew is different. He is loud. He is reactionary. He invades your personal space. He gets to wear headphones at school. He likes The Wiggles and Disney, Jr. He takes Buzz Lightyear with him everywhere he can. He chews on his clothes and bites his fingernails. He picks his nose; frankly, so do some of you, but you are just more sleuth about it than he is. He pulls the strings off of his socks. He speaks out in class. He is autistic. In medical terms, "Autism is a developmental disorder characterized by difficulties with social interaction and communication and by restricted and repetitive behavior." In simpler words, his brain works a little differently than yours and mine, but differently is not less!

Sometimes you focus on the things that are different or that you do not understand in a person, and you miss out on so much. With Matthew, it means you do not know that he loves pizza and mac and cheese just as much as you do. You might not know that he has been able to say his ABCs backwards since he was four, or that he can remember tiny details about movies that the rest of us forget before we leave the theater. He loves music and is learning to play piano. He can swim. He would wear a bowtie to school every day if it was in the dress code. He likes to bake. He takes great pictures. He loves to go to middle school dances. He LOVES screens: iPad, computer, phone, DVD player, you name it. Loves them and can figure out things about them without being taught, just like you. He loves Disney Pixar movies, especially all of the Toy Story movies. He can repeat most of Toy Story 2 word for word as you watch it. And he wants to have friends; he just does not always know how.

You may not know that there are reasons for most of the strange things he does. He is super sensitive to noise and is deathly afraid of fire drills, so he wears headphones in school just in case. He bites his fingernails because he is always anxious at school. He is anxious because school is a major struggle for him, he has to adjust to all of the unexpected sounds, changes in schedule, the workload. He has to do homework, like you. It looks a little different than yours, but is equally challenging for him. He goes to therapy after school to learn to do the things that come more naturally to you. He is afraid of fire, even the candles at church scare him. We do not know why, but they do. Sometimes he does know the answer to the question you just asked, but before he can find the words, you have moved on to something or someone else. He processes verbal language more slowly than you and I do, but processes things on screen really quickly. He is easily distracted, like by a fly on the window. If he tells you he sees or hears something, you should believe him even if you cannot see or hear it. Trust me, he is usually correct, especially when it comes to bugs and snakes. He does not do so well in PE because it is loud and overstimulating and he has poor motor skills, so his coordination is not as good as yours. He would like to play some of those games you play, but they move too fast for him and he gets frustrated.

I am grateful that Matthew attends school at Sacred Heart Cathedral School, where kindness and inclusion are taught and encouraged. I wish we found those values more often at the grocery store and the park. And while I started writing this note to teenagers, I have realized that there are takeaways for all of us. Be kind, share a smile or a kind word when you pass. If you see someone sitting alone at lunch or church, ask if you can join them.

I hope that you give Matthew, or someone like Matthew, a chance. Take the time it takes to get to know them. Try to find something you have in common, whether it is pizza or Disney Pixar. Middle school life is tough whether you are the cool kid or not, so take a chance and make a new friend. A little kindness goes a long way, and everyone can use some more kindness in his world.

Thank you,

Mrs. Mommy

[6] If you are so inclined, she is on XM radio 129 from 1-3 pm Central time, Monday through Friday.

[7] sites.psu.edu/astrowright/2015/06/02/imposter-syndrome

10

Matthew's Village

The Ripple Effect

A ripple effect can be described as a situation in which one event causes a series of other events to happen. Lately, I have been reflecting on the ripples that Matthew's life has caused in the lives of those around us.

One of the first people to come to mind was our dear friend Caroline. We met Caroline and her parents the first week we moved to Pensacola. When Matthew arrived in 2004, Angela was an easy choice to be Matthew's godmother, so the relationship deepened. Caroline babysat for us beginning in the summer of 2002, she watched the big kids grow up and developed a special relationship with Matthew. Her patience with him was extraordinary. In the early years, it was difficult to trust sitters with him, and Caroline set the standard for everyone else.

We all cried when Caroline left for the University of Florida. She began her college career as a Public Relations major, but during her spring semester a career interest test suggested she might excel in speech pathology and special education. She took a class and developed a love for speech and language, with a special passion for working with people with autism. She called me often, asking about "my Matthew" and telling me stories of children who reminded her of him. She worked with him when she came home for the summer. She shared research studies with me. She led the UF fundraiser "Stomp the Swamp" for autism, all for the love of Matthew.

Fast forward a few years and two states later to 10:54 pm on a Tuesday night, when she texted me saying she is "officially co-owner and partner of a speech language pathology practice." Amazing! I knew Caroline would do great things, no matter what field she chose, but it fills my heart to see the great things she is doing to help those who learn things differently or with great difficulty. See the ripple?.

And then there is Mrs. Robinson, Matthew's after school caregiver. She is like a member of the family. I truly don't know what we would do without her. We met Rhonda in first grade at Cordova Park. She was a "parent educator" assigned to support Matthew, and a beautiful relationship began. After she moved on to a new school, I asked her to consider working with Matthew after school. She was very successful at getting Matthew to do his best work. She sees Matthew's gifts and encourages him to use them. She loves him like he is her child, yet she doesn't let him use autism as an excuse for poor behavior or bad choices. She doesn't just love Matthew though; she loves all children. She has a passion for working with children who don't have the same parental support Matthew does or the access to services that Matthew does.

One day, Rhonda told me that she had decided to pursue a degree in speech pathology. Her work with Matthew was leading her to work with others as well. She continued to work with Matthew after school, while pursuing a new degree. Rhonda will be a wonderful speech therapist. She has the patience of Job. She has a heart of gold. She wants to make a difference, and she will. Another ripple.

These ripple effects—these subtle. or not so subtle, changes in lives because of Matthew or the impact of Matthew and children like him—fill my heart. Every day in this world we cross paths with others and we may never know just how much our simple gestures impact someone's life. We may never know that how we handled adversity gave someone else hope or courage. Our challenge and how we face it can set or change the course for someone else. Sometimes we are fortunate enough to witness the ripple.

A Picture is Worth a Thousand Words

Many times, pictures convey things that words can't or don't adequately describe. This picture (taken by Priscilla Gail Teal) is my favorite of Matthew and Grand Bowers, my mom. It captures their relationship so well. She recently began to call him "her shadow," and while it is appropriate for him, it could likewise be appropriate for her. They would follow each other to the ends of the earth. I have pondered how to properly thank her for the extraordinary love she shows Matthew and haven't found the right words. So I will simply say, "Thank You, Grand!" and let the picture say the rest.

Grand and her "shadow" (photo credit: Priscilla Gail Teal, edited by Kim Bernstein)

It Takes a Village

Hillary Clinton once wrote a book entitled "It Takes a Village" about things we learn from raising children. I did not read the book, but I think the title perfectly sums up what is required to raise children, autistic or not. As a result of Matthew's diagnosis, our village has grown exponentially over the years. It started off small with family and close friends, and it has grown to include speech therapists, occupational therapists, behavioral therapists, pediatric neuropsychologists, pediatric neurologists, teachers, paraprofessionals, and tutors to name a few. Some of the villagers move in and out over the years; some leave by choice, and others you have to ask to leave.

In a fairly brief span of time, you learn who believes in your child and the lengths they are willing to go to help them achieve success. One of the professionals who has been there since the beginning and who I consider indispensable to our village is Matthew's pediatric neuropsychologist, Karen Hagerott, PhD. She has seen us laugh and cry. She has guided us through difficult decisions, But the thing that sticks with me most is that she always presumes Matthew's competence. Even in the early years, when Matthew didn't make eye contact or couldn't answer her questions, Dr. Hagerott spent time in every appointment asking him meaningful questions and waiting patiently for his response. She has been instrumental in helping us find the next therapist, or school, or book to guide us.

We are also grateful for the role that his second through fifth grade teachers Fran Zayszly and Darla Creeks have played in Matthew's life. There aren't words to describe the growth Matthew has experienced under them. When he walked into their classroom years ago, his academic and social progress took a different turn. They presume competence in all of their students and encourage them to believe they can do anything. They are not "just" teachers, they are therapists, advocates, surrogate moms, disciplinarians, and now, lifelong friends.

Super Heroes

For months, we planned a spring break trip to Texas to visit our Bowers cousins. We prepared Matthew in a variety of ways: we talked, we looked at pictures of his aunt and uncle and five cousins, we practiced names, we talked some more. Excitement built for Matthew; he loves a good road trip with a different Hampton Inn every night along the way. I must admit that I experienced a little nervousness. There were no reasons at all for the nerves; my brother's family is one of the most loving, big-hearted, accepting-of-all-kind of family anyone could ask for.

We last visited with them in Pensacola over a year ago and they moved into a new home since we last travelled to Texas.

I wasn't sure how much Matthew would remember. I knew he would be curious and want to explore their new home. We prepared in the car during the last part of our drive; we talked about appropriate behaviors in someone else's home, what to touch, what not to touch, and so on. When we arrived, the cousins immediately took Matthew on the grand tour, letting him explore and touch. Their beautiful new home looks like it was styled by Joanna Gaines AND is Matthew friendly! He made himself at home in the playroom, loving their vintage, canvas toy box on wheels!

The adults visited in the living room, when we heard laughter and children playing in the next room; One of the voices belonged to Matthew and the other to his cousin Jeb. I jumped up to take a look and confirm I heard correctly, that it was happy play. I snuck up to the doorway and soaked in the moment. Matthew playing, really playing, with another child. Sweet Jeb, wise beyond his years at six, playing right along with Matthew. They laughed out loud and negotiated; I couldn't understand quite what they were saying. They moved from one part of the room to another, completely engaged and unaware of anything else. For a moment, my eyes welled up, grateful to Jeb for accepting Matthew and playing along, grateful to witness this snapshot of normalcy, grateful to God for allowing me to witness the joy they shared. I ran for my camera and videoed for a minute; they didn't even know I was there.

A little later in the afternoon, I noticed Matthew and Jeb found their way back to one other. Sitting on the couch, watching Toy Story 2 on the iPad. The quiet moment was in sharp contrast to the earlier exchange. I asked my niece to snap a quick picture, so I could remember the special moment later. I think the picture speaks a thousand words.

I tried to convey to my brother and his older children the enormity of these exchanges, but I'm not sure I did them justice. Matthew tries to engage other kids at times, but many don't have the patience necessary to play with him or willingness to participate in the movie talk he requests. I'm not sure I succeeded at explaining my appreciation and gratitude not just for this interaction, but for how amazing all of the cousins were with Matthew all day long. Their love for someone who didn't think like they did, or speak like they did, shone through. Thank you, Chase and Laura for raising children who know how to love!

Tonight, as we settled down for bed, I asked Matthew what game he and Jeb were playing. He said, "We were pretend super heroes; Jeb was Fireman and I was Waterman and we were fighting. He was shooting fire at things, and I was trying to put his fire out with water blasts. It was fun!" Matthew and Jeb, you boys *are* super heroes. For the different battles you fight every day. Jeb, you are Aunt Rocky's super hero on so many levels: for your own story, for your unabashed acceptance of Matthew and willingness to meet him where he is, and for your love of life which radiates from your beautiful soul.

She Was Right There All the Time

To say that Cordova Park exceeded our expectations for Elementary School would be an understatement! Of course, hindsight is 20/20, and looking back at what made it special was not the location or the facilities or the convenience. It was the people. Teachers like Mrs. Brown, Mrs. Stevens, Mrs. Killam, Ms. Creek and the amazing Mrs. Fran Zayszly. Therapists like Brandt Thorn and Mrs. Voeltz, who patiently waited for Matthew and I in the carline in all kinds of weather. Paraprofessionals like Mrs. Robinson, Ms. Lovelace and Ms. Cooper. All of admin and support: Ms. Bauer, Ms. Cooper, Ms. Herren, Ms. Liz in the clinic and on and on… they all grew to love Matthew.

Then there were the children—the ones who grew up with Matthew, who treated him with such kindness and patience—Chad, Giselle, Natalie, Nathan, Darius. I could list so many more. There are even more that I couldn't name, but they were so kind, they spoke to Matthew, they played with him, they helped him around school. They learned about autism, and they raced past awareness into acceptance.

I must admit that I experienced a lot of apprehension when we made the decision to place Matthew at Sacred Heart Cathedral School in the Morning Star program. I asked myself lots of questions, but the most prevailing were, "How would the children respond to him? Would he have any friends?" Our family knew other families with children at the school, but as far as I knew, Matthew didn't really know other children at the school.

On the "meet the teacher" day, we cautiously walked down the long hall to one of the sixth-grade homeroom classes. Matthew would share inclusion activities with this group of students when he was not in Morning Star classes. I was so afraid he wouldn't know anyone. When we walked in, I quickly scanned the room for a familiar face. I felt a sigh of relief when I saw other moms that I knew. There was even one young man Matthew had been in kindergarten and first grade with at Cordova Park. Suddenly, a petite girl with long hair walked up and began speaking to Matthew. Her mom introduced herself to me and explained that her daughter, Cailey, had gone to school with Matthew at Cordova Park. She went on to tell me that Cailey sat next to him in Math or Science and was a buddy to him. Cailey was happy to continue to be a helper to Matthew at SHCS; she volunteered to be there for him because he was her friend. I felt both overwhelming gratitude and guilt. Gratitude for this amazing kindness she extended to Matthew, and guilt for not knowing about her during our time at Cordova Park.

I left that day feeling like it was going to be okay. Sweet Cailey was such a friend to Matthew from August to December. She escorted him to the car in the afternoons for carline, she played with him on the playground, she looked out for him. At the end of December, her family moved to another school, and SHCS was not quite the same without her. I thought about her almost every day when Matthew walked to the car alone. While I was thankful for his newfound independence, I missed the friendship he shared with Cailey, and I believe he did as well. There are other children who are kind to him, but they don't share the history with him that Cailey did. Hopefully, they one day will.

A while ago, I was looking through some photos, and I came across the one pictured above. As soon as I saw it, I immediately paused. Guess who was right by Matthew's side in this picture from his fourth-grade recorder concert at Cordova Park Elementary? Sweet Cailey. I had probably looked at this picture at least twenty times since it was taken, but I never knew who the girl next to him was. Well, now I know; Cailey was right there all along. Before she left SHCS, I did my best to express my thanks to her. I hope that one day she understands what a big impression her kindness made on me and on Matthew.

Teachers Have Superpowers!

If you do the math, teachers often spend as much time (or more) with our children during the school age years as we do. When things are going well for one child in the class, they might not be for another. Teachers have to have special powers to balance the needs of the children in their classroom. That's any teacher, and when you throw special needs children into that classroom, it's like juggling with one hand. You can be in the fanciest school and have an ill-equipped teacher or in the poorest school with a rock star teacher.

We've been very fortunate over the years to have some amazing teachers work with Matthew. Each of them seemed to be just what he needed at the time. They morph into mind readers, translators, therapists, behavior coaches, nurses—all this on top of teaching their students. They work long hours for little pay, hoping to see their rewards in student success—inside and outside of the classroom. They sacrifice their time and time with their families to ensure the preparation of our students.

The parent-teacher relationship requires work by both parties, even more so when a special needs child is involved. Good, honest communication makes the relationship more solid. As a special needs parent, you must have faith in the abilities of your child's teachers. "Teachers change the world one life at a time," sums up the impact one great teacher can have on a family. Great teachers don't just lift up the student, they lift up the whole family. Each new skill taught and mastered opens new doors and new possibilities.

In a recent conversation, Matthew's teacher shared a story with me that warmed my heart and strengthened my faith in her. She recounted a recent episode where a younger student asked her why Matthew always wears headphones. In my mind, I thought of my typical answer to that question: Introduction to Autism 101, which results in a glazed over look from the child as she walks away. Her answer was not boring; instead it was brilliant. She explained that Matthew has "superpower-like" hearing, and he hears sounds that we don't. She compared it to how certain animals have a keen sense of smell or a super hero that has x-ray vision. She told the child how Matthew can hear a fly buzz in the corner of a room when we don't even know the fly is there. She's right; if Matthew says he can hear something, anything, he's not lying. The young man walked away satisfied and a bit impressed with Matthew's superpowers.

The other student was not nearly as impressed as I was by Mrs. Susann's superpowers: quick thinking and a wonderful, truthful explanation of why Matthew wears headphones. Insightful honesty about a "strength" instead of excusing a "challenge." The positive spin may change how that young man looks at others who don't quite fit the norm. Matthew's day can be derailed by a fly or a fluorescent light losing its power (very high-pitched sound) or the air conditioner turning off and on or a fire drill; it's a struggle. Simple sounds that don't even garner our attention create constant distractions for him. The headphones muffle the sounds just enough to lessen their distraction but do not prevent Matthew from hearing his teachers. As I walked away with a smile on my face, I thought that not only does Matthew have superpowers, but this teacher does too! Thank you to all those teachers who have used their superpowers to help Matthew become the best version of himself.

Making Music

Matthew has loved music and instruments for as long as I can remember. He gravitates to movies and TV shows with music or singing like The Wiggles, The Backyardigans and Little Einsteins. He likes to listen to classical music in the car. He keeps miniatures of instruments in his treasure box. He fixates on tubas anytime we see them.

Over the years, we made several attempts to teach him an instrument. We bought a child's cello at an auction, but then could not find anyone willing to teach him. We ultimately donated the cello to a non-profit. We bought a tuba from Goodwill. He loved it so much, but he couldn't figure out the breathing techniques necessary to play it. That instrument received a lot of love from Matthew before it "retired" from service. He participated in the Cordova Strings program during his fifth-grade year at CPE and it was successful due to an amazing strings teacher, Ms. Clark, and an assist from our beloved Ms. Creek. Ms. Creek attended every class with him and played hand over hand with him. His fine motors skills limited his ability to play violin by himself and led to frustration on his part, so we scratched the violin. I kept my ears open hoping to find just the right music teacher for Matthew.

Recently, my friend Jessica shared a link to **Melody Makers 850** advertising a local adaptive music teacher, Mrs. Stephanie. I immediately reached out to her to inquire about piano lessons for Matthew. Our first conversation put my mind at ease, I knew she was well qualified to work with adaptive students and more importantly, was enthusiastic about working with Matthew, specifically.

I asked Matthew if he wanted to take piano lessons and he quickly replied, "Yes, when do we start?" I made arrangements for an initial lesson and prayed for the best. I hate to admit that in an out-of-character fashion for me, I did no further research or homework on the program. I just relied on my friend's recommendation and God's divine intervention.

Upon meeting Mrs. Stephanie and observing her interacting with Matthew, my expectations rose a bit. The program involves teaching the students to read and play music using a combination of color-coded handbells, videos, workbooks and of course, a keyboard or piano. To both of our surprise, we learned that Matthew possesses pretty solid pitch. He identified notes by ear, that I had no idea he knew. He loved playing the bells and channeling his inner Ord, from Dragon Tales, and shouting "Dooooo!" Lesson 1 ended with excitement on my part and anticipation on Matthew's. I believed we finally found the right music teacher for Matthew and he practiced and prepared for the next lesson without complaint.

After ten weeks of lessons, Matthew was practicing without much of a push from me. His pitch continues to improve. His fingers are growing stronger and his motor skills are improving. He's adding some root notes with the left hand and still managing to play the right. I'm so proud of him and he's prouder of himself. He's looking ahead in the songbook, anxious to get to some of his favorites from The Wiggles. I'm grateful to Mrs. Stephanie for her patience and persistence. I'm grateful to whoever created this program that makes sense to my son, who doesn't always learn things the straightforward way. A bonus is that I am learning to read music, too! Just one more lesson I never expected to learn from Matthew.

11

"But I Don't Want To Go To School"

A Test of My Patience

Let me just say this right up front: I am NOT a fan of high-stakes testing! While I understand the need for periodic, standardized testing, as piece of each child's academic portfolio, I am not in favor of the role of state-based, standardized testing in schools today. The stress this testing creates for administrators (at the school and district level), teachers, parents, and students is counterproductive to the ultimate goal of educating our children. The stress exists for most students, neuro-typical and neuro-diverse students, gifted, average or intellectually disabled students. For Matthew and other students with IEPs or 504 plans, testing presents another wrinkle. For those of you who aren't familiar with IEPs or 504s, these documents guide the students' academic plan for the upcoming year. They include what support the student receives, one on one or a part-time aide or small group instruction; they also include any accommodations a student receives like extra time for testing or a different colored paper or any tools they are allowed to use like a keyboard to type instead of write. Without getting into too many details, Matthew requires quite a few accommodations. However, with the accommodations, like extra time and typing in lieu of writing, he experiences less frustration and more success. The unfortunate thing is that many of the accommodations he uses on an everyday basis for classroom work and school-based testing do not apply for state-based testing or "high stakes" testing. Yes, he gets additional time and someone makes sure that his blanks are intentional (that he didn't get off track in his bubbling). Sometimes if we are lucky, if he needs paper-based, he gets paper-based or he might get to use a computer. Other times he does not get whet he needs. All of this makes my head spin and makes him a little anxious, because just like any other student, he wants to do well.

So, we plan, we work, we practice and we bribe. Did I say bribe? I meant reward! Matthew is autistic and ADHD; the combination of those two diagnoses contribute to challenging testing conditions. Keeping him on track, so that he actually benefits from the extra time he is allowed, can be undermined by his autistic tendencies to look at material from his specific perspective of the subject and not the more general one intended by the test preparers. So, his team plans and offers rewards, not for his outcomes, but for his efforts. Tuesday it was cake. He wanted a cake—not a little cake, not a cupcake, but a real cake. So, Tuesday afternoon I received a text with the picture above from his teacher. The students get to write their name on the board each day they complete the testing process doing their best and at the end of the testing (three weeks) those who do well earn a ticket to a Star Wars Party. His teacher told him to go write his name for Tuesday because he was a Rockstar! So that's what he wrote: "Matthew is a Rockstar." When I opened the text, my heart filled with emotion. I want the bureaucrats who make the rules about testing to SEE the children who do not fit into that plan. I want them to understand that just because their test doesn't match Matthew's way of thinking doesn't mean he can't be successful in a traditional school setting with his peers. Yes, the test can be one piece, but his academic work in the classroom, his therapeutic progress and his desire to learn should also factor into the decision.

Guess what? After testing on Tuesday Matthew chose cake at *Fresh Market* with strawberries on top. (Side note: The really nice lady in the bakery at Fresh Market heard Matthew say he wanted a cake with strawberries, only the cake he really wanted did not have any. She came around to him and told him she would add strawberries to the cake he chose. She got it and I love her for that!) We had a pretend surprise birthday party, we went through our nighttime routine and we prepared for Wednesday's testing. The "reward" for good choices on Wednesday: a DVD in the mail. The "great" report arrived on Wednesday. Matthew came home went straight to the computer and found his reward, a Wiggles DVD. Easy, right? Wrong! He found a Wiggles TV episode on the Australian version of iTunes called "A Picnic Without Ants" and it is NOT available for US iTunes or DVD players. Fun times.

I would love for you all to please think of how we can affect change in our educational system to make testing an appropriate piece of the system, not the driving force. This would not only impact students like Matthew; it affects all of our kids.

Decisions, Decisions

Brett and I prayerfully prepared to make a decision about middle school for Matthew. To understand the difficulty of this decision, you need to know where we started. Matthew began his preschool education at age two at the First Methodist Church Mother's Day Out Program in Pensacola. Sometime during that year, during his diagnosis process, it occurred to us that he needed greater support and services than this wonderful, traditional preschool provided. I started a quest for the "right" developmental preschool. I wanted everything in a school for Matthew that the school my older children attended had to offer. I wanted it to look like a school, I wanted the class parties and letters of the week. I looked at the public-school offerings, all in lower-income neighborhoods, full of children who needed so much support. Not simple things, like speech therapy and behavioral therapy, but complicated things like transportation from foster care, consistent meals, family support. I realized that while the administrators, teachers and professional therapists in these schools were highly qualified, their plates were overflowing with children with greater needs than Matthew's.

Another mom I met at Speech Therapy, suggested I take a look at Capstone Academy. Capstone, a charter school, provided an inclusive educational learning opportunity for children with a spectrum of abilities and disabilities. As a bonus, it looked like a school and felt like a school. To this mom, struggling with accepting her child's diagnosis and trying to formulate a plan to meet his ever-growing needs, Capstone was a breath of fresh air.Mr. Thomas, the principal, put me at ease and assured me that Capstone was right for Matthew. Matthew spent two glorious years at Capstone. He experienced immense progress while enjoying some of the traditional fun of preschool, all the while I fixated on the next decision. Where would we go for elementary school?

As the search for an elementary school began, I learned new vocabulary words: IEPs, 504 plans, funding matrices, paraprofessionals and Wright's Law. I discovered that my role as a mom was sometimes secondary to my role as advocate.I visited private elementary schools and none seemed to fit Matthew's needs. At a time where "low-functioning" and "high-functioning" were still politically correct terms, my "middle-functioning" child did not seem to fit anywhere. I shifted my focus to public alternatives. School district officials encouraged me to visit a public school in our area that had all the services Matthew needed in lieu of our home school. Thinking that they were the "professionals," I agreed to a visit.Once again, I found a school where many of the children's needs exceeded far beyond Matthew's and I believed he would get lost in the shuffle. On a whim, I decided to visit our districted, "neighborhood" elementary school, Cordova Park Elementary (CPE).

I approached the meeting with the Principal with fear and trepidation. I wanted this traditional elementary experience so much, both for Matthew and for myself. Aggie Bauer welcomed me to our meeting and patiently listened to all of my concerns, hopes, and fears.... Then, to my surprise, she said she thought we could make this work. She established an open, honest working relationship with me from Day 1 and for that I am eternally grateful. For the past six years, school administration, the teachers, the therapists, the support staff and most importantly, the students welcomed, accepted and loved Matthew more than I could have imagined. It hasn't been without challenges; we have laughed, cried, made plans, changed plans, all the while working together. Matthew enjoyed inclusion settings for K-2, and then Fran Zayszly arrived at CPE. Matthew moved into a varying exceptionality classroom for some subjects and continued inclusion for others through fifth grade. When Matthew started elementary school, I never dreamed his experience would be so "normal." I am so grateful for how much love we felt at CPE.

Then it was time to graduate from Cordova Park.

Middle School—the big decision. Once again, I visited private schools, public schools, charter schools. The choices were difficult. In elementary school, Matthew participated in general education curriculum, mostly on grade level with his IEP accommodations. In middle school, staying Gen Ed becomes a bigger challenge. Once you leave Gen Ed and the diploma track, it is difficult, if not impossible to get back on. We weren't ready to leave that track.

At one point, I walked into a school, immense Matthew packet in hand, had an "aha" moment and thought the search was over. But then we learned that the school did not think they could meet Matthew's needs. So, the quest continued. I was down to one school, patiently waiting for an invitation to tour and if that did not work out, well... I did what I always do whenever we face difficult Matthew-related decisions, I visited our neuropsychologist Dr. Hagerott. As usual, she had a plan. She encouraged us to wait to find out if that one school had a place for Matthew. However, if they did not have a spot, she encouraged me to—wait for it—home school until they did. Home School? Wait—doesn't she know I said, "I would never home school?"

We all know that God doesn't sleep and has a great sense of humor, and Dr. Hagerott believes in my abilities more than I do. I walked out with a plan.

The Lost Boys (and Girls)

I try to be as transparent as possible when it comes to writing about our family's experience with autism. I try to be honest without betraying Matthew's privacy or writing things I think he might find hurtful when he reads them at some point in the future. I also want to remind readers that this is just one family's experience with autism—I don't want to presume to speak on behalf of the community. Just like if you know one child with autism, you only "know" one child with autism; the same could be said for the family.

Despite different family experiences, there are common challenges we all face. The looming question for us right now concerns Matthew's future education. It seems absurd to me that we are faced with deciding whether he can continue to pursue a traditional high school diploma before he finishes 6th grade, a full ten years until he ages out of services at the end of the academic year he turns 22 years old. Yet, here we are at such a crossroads.

In elementary school, Matthew participated in a blend of general education and resource classes. He received accommodations and scaffolding where indicated and made a lot of progress in math and science. Reading comprehension, especially fiction-based material, presents major challenges for him, mostly due to his inability to fully understand abstract concepts. Standardized testing and end of course exams, which do not allow for accommodations beyond extended time, and include lots of word problems, do not align with Matthew's strengths.

In an effort to find the right balance of social and academic opportunity for Matthew, we selected a private middle school for him. We learned over the course of this year, that while Matthew made great social gains in school, his academic progress waned. So back to the crossroads. Now we must re-evaluate our school decision and our options. So, it appears, in Escambia County, in Pensacola, Florida, we have options for those who need full ESE services and we have options for those who can succeed in a fully-inclusive general education setting, but limited options for those who fall somewhere in between, the lost boys. (Yes, girls too, but for my purpose, we will discuss boys).

We face difficult decisions about whether he can continue to pursue a traditional diploma. I am perplexed. We have a child showing a continued capacity to learn, just at a slower pace. There's just not a slower-pace option. We must craft our own within rules that weren't written with us in mind. Make it up as we go, frightening for this Type A kind of girl. We can repeat years, but we can't spread one year into two. We can't really individualize the education and stay within the system. We can home school, but that is not really a good choice for someone who needs social skills practice and neuro-typical peers. I know we aren't the only family facing this dilemma; with 1 in 68 children on the spectrum and 1 in 42 boys having ASD, lots of families face this dilemma.

We need creativity, we need to re-think the path, and we need parents and special education teachers involved in forging a path for the lost boys. This needs to be a path that leads to a diploma, or a vocational skill or industry certification that prepares these children and young adults for whatever level of independence they can achieve. We need a Plan B. Right now, we are parents scrambling to piece together, a school program, and a therapy plan and anything else we can find, to solve this puzzle. This keeps me up at night, and I think my friends in the autism community will read this and nod, because it keeps them up at night, too. For now, I will research, advocate, and pray for the ability to discern the right educational path for Matthew and hope that we come to a better solution for Matthew and those like him.

Are We on the Right Path?

As a special needs parent, and really as a typical parent too, there are days where you question if you are on the right path. Are you making the right decisions for or with your children? Are you providing them with the "right" therapies, the "right" opportunities, the "right" school? Where you need a sign (or two) to continue the fight, I mean the path, or to scrap it and move to Plan B.

This afternoon, I was having one of those days with Matthew. When he got into the car after school, he was very distraught because he had made a "poor choice" at school. His communication challenges made it difficult for me to fully understand what had transpired and how to proceed. We had a long talk about the situation and how he could do better next time. He wrote a note of apology. I wrestled with myself and my choices. About that time his new teacher called to talk to me about his day. On Friday afternoon, when she could have sent an email or started her weekend with her own family, she took the time to call me. She reassured me about how well he recovered from his misstep and then went on to describe their breakthrough today. What seemed like a disaster to Matthew led to real progress in her eyes. She saw the "giant leap" of what might have looked like "baby steps" to a bystander. I was grateful for her phone call and for her insight and her desire to meet Matthew where he is.

We were set to conclude our day with Fun Friday at SEASTARS Aquatics, where Matthew is on the swim team. One Friday of each month, the entire team gathers for social time. Matthew LOVES Fun Friday and counts the number of sleeps until the next one. Matthew brought his mono fin, but the miracle worker Coach Robin convinced him to play with friends instead. He rallied, swam and played with his teammates for almost an hour. It's a beautiful sight to see these teammates of all ages, races, ethnicities and abilities just enjoying the water and each other. Then, to our surprise, Matthew was named "Swimmer of the Week!" He was recognized for his hard work this year and for his improvement. With a lot of encouragement from Coach Robin and Coach Gracie, Matthew has made great strides in his swimming this past year. They challenge him and encourage him to go outside his comfort zone; they meet him where he is.

I am grateful for the signs today. I am grateful for this boy, this young man who challenges me every day to meet him where he is and further to help him become the best possible version of himself.

Dance(ing) to the Beat of His Own Drum

As the parent of a child with developmental delays, there are days that you don't expect to come or milestones you don't plan to experience with your child. It's not that you don't hope for these events—you do, you just don't count on them. When milestones are reached, timely or not, you celebrate them.

One afternoon as I drove Matthew home from school, we talked about his day and his excitement that it was Friday and there was no school the next day. Like most days he described it as "excellent" and immediately asked for his iPad. Then he surprised me. He asked if he could go to school tomorrow "to the dance."

"What dance? There's a dance?" I asked. Actually, I knew there was a middle school dance; I just had not considered that he might want to go. I had known about the dance since that Wednesday when Matthew and I took pictures of the advertisement poster for the dance to be posted on the school blog. I assumed that it would be too loud, too dark, possibly not too welcoming. But Matthew went on to explain that there was a dance at his school on Saturday night and that he wanted to go and he was going to dance with his friend Zoe.

My heart dropped. He was excited about this dance and had a plan. I wanted to explain that it might not be so simple, that it might be overwhelming, that the other kids might not welcome him, that I was afraid of what could go wrong, but I didn't. Instead, I told him we would talk to Dad. When I told Brett of Matthew's request, he was thrilled. He said, "Let him go. We'll drop him off and go have some dinner! He'll be fine." Of course, I thought Brett was crazy and listed all of my concerns: we didn't have a plan, I didn't know if the Morning Star students go to the dances, would his teacher be there, what if it was a disaster, and so on. But there was a tug on my heart that I should support this request, that I should help Matthew get to that dance, but my head, oh how my head was arguing with my heart.

Saturday morning, Matthew still insisted he wanted to attend the dance and Brett was still encouraging this craziness. I reluctantly texted two other Morning Star moms and they said, "Of course, Morning Star students are invited!" Yikes. and yes, their kids were going, but they would likely be there as well, just in case. So, I decided we would do this: I would take him to the dance and then hide, ready to swoop in if he needed me or if things went south.

After mass but before the dance, Brett reminded me to "presume competence" and I didn't believe that I wasn't, but in retrospect, he was likely correct (don't tell him I admitted it!).

Matthew picked out a dapper outfit— plaid flannel pants, white shirt and red bowtie (and color coordinating headphones) —and we headed to school. On the way, we talked about do's and don'ts: asking girls to dance, respecting their answer if they decline, giving people personal space, etc... When we drove into the parking lot, my heart dropped; there were a lot of kids, and they weren't just from Sacred Heart Cathedral School, but also St. Paul Catholic School, Creative Learning Academy and Episcopal Day School. I wanted to turn around and head home, to save him (and me) from whatever might be behind those doors, but we kept putting one foot in front of the other. At the front door, one of his classmates said with great surprise in his voice, "Matthew Parra, welcome to the dance!"

Immediately we faced our first obstacle: decorative balloons! Matthew stopped in his tracks; he fears balloons. Actually, he fears the sound of balloons popping. I assured him they would not pop. He dropped his admission money at the entrance table and took off for the gym.

The music blared, strobe lights flashed, lots of middle schoolers clustered around the room and Matthew took off into the crowd to dance. I sought a familiar face of another special needs parent and waited with her. Waited for him to return, worried about what he was doing or who he was talking to or dancing with. It didn't take long to learn from his teacher (Thank God she was there!) that he was dancing (with girls!!), enjoying cookies and overcoming challenges with every step he took. He came to check on me (for just a minute) and the joy on his face was priceless: he was having fun just like every other child in the room. Actually, he was probably having more fun than lots of the kids in the room. He wasn't worried about what anyone thought about how he danced, who he danced with, or what outfit he had on. He just danced, embraced the moment and had a blast. Then a balloon popped and he was done. He found his teacher and told her he was ready to go and find mom.

I almost cried, a few times, when I let myself think about the enormity of the night. For many parents, a middle school dance is a blip on the radar, but for Matthew (and for me—who are we kidding), this was a big deal. For him to communicate something that he wanted to do (that was out of the norm) with his typical peers, thrive in an extremely challenging sensory environment, determine when to leave on his own and then talk about it afterwards was HUGE! I was so proud of him. My take away was to listen more closely to the things he wants to do and not discount them as too difficult or impossible. I need to take my own advice; I need to be the example and presume competence.

Back to School

Back to school; a simple phrase that evokes images of the freshly stocked school supply aisles at Target, the fun of shopping for new school clothes or uniforms, the excitement of selecting a backpack or lunchbox for the coming year, and the obligatory first day of school picture. In our household, and many others with special needs children, "back to school" conjures myriad additional and different emotions and images. Where will we find a lunchbox that is age-appropriate but also beloved? Will the school supplies required accommodate my child's sensory needs? Do the uniforms come in elastic waist? Can we find shoes that meet the school requirements in a slip-on version?

Matthew started counting how many sleeps until school starts the day after school ended for summer (75 sleeps of summer to be exact.) Unfortunately, the countdown was not one driven by the excitement of returning to school; instead, it was driven by the anxiety of returning to school. The anxiety does not end with Matthew; I experience it as well. In my most anxious moments, I stop and pray for God's peace and guidance.

With each new school year, there are lots of changes. The changes are not just schedule changes, but also classmate and teacher changes. Fortunately for us, Matthew is part of the Morning Star program at Sacred Heart Cathedral School, where students are "inspired to be servant leaders to one another" and some students put that inspiration into action. I am comforted when he hops out of the car and is greeted with smiles by special friends who ensure he has someone to eat lunch with and play with on the playground. I am reminded that these friends are the hands and feet of Jesus when they care for Matthew. I am comforted by the beauty I find in the midst of Matthew's challenges.

The sensory challenges that accompany Matthew's autism make school a challenge for him in a variety of ways. For all children, autistic or not, school is work and not play, and while it can be fun, it is not exactly designed to be fun. For Matthew, however, that's just the beginning. There's the change of routine. Routine and order are important for him—in all aspects of his life. Matthew wants to know what is going to happen and when. He will memorize the schedule by day and any unannounced deviation can affect his mood and ability to participate. The schedule exists but does not always play out the way it looks on paper. Until he can have a week or two of normalcy in the schedule, Matthew is not fully able to adjust to the change from summer. As a result of the chaos, we typically see a regression in behavior and an intensity of his autistic tendencies. During these challenging times, I look for refuge. The lyrics of my favorite hymn, *On Eagle's Wings*, are a place of refuge. I find great peace in the verses of this song and related scripture. I know God is with me during these moments of change and chaos.

We've been blessed with great teachers, like Fran Zayszly in elementary school and Diana Susann and Julie Lippincott Schuck at SHCS, who take great pride in meeting each student where they are and trying to get the most out of them. It's reassuring to know that there are teachers who write notes home, send countless texts of reassurance and reminder emails on the weekend, understand the difference between autism and bad behavior, and see their work as a calling and reflect that in their words and deeds.

I know each new school year brings change and change is hard, but ultimately change is good. One day, not so far away, Matthew's time in school will pass and he will have to find his place in the world. He will "go to college" (like his older siblings) or a vocational program or get a job. He will have to make new friends and work for people who do not know anything about him or autism. Every day I pray that all of the changes and challenges that accompany the back to school season are preparation for the changes and challenges that accompany the next season of life.

The Good Choices Book

One day on the ride home from school, Matthew and I were discussing his choices that day and what he could or should have done differently. I asked him point blank, "What do you think would help you make better choices? I know you can make the right choices, but it seems like you forget to sometimes."

He first said, "I don't know" with some resignation. He sat quietly for a moment and then he said, "I've got it. I could make good choices if I had a **Good Choices** book to remind me."

I thought for a quick second and asked Matthew if he could write one for himself or if he needed my help. He reflected and said, "I can do it." As soon as we arrived home from school, I found a small notebook and presented it to him. He exclaimed it was "perfect" and set to work. He wrote out all the school rules in his head:

1. No Yelling!
2. No Hitting!
3. No saying **bad** words!
4. No saying, "I don't want to go!"
5. No being mean!
6. No knocking down chairs! (In Matthew's world this involves walking over to the chair, looking someone in the eye and laying the chair on its side on the floor, not actually flipping the chair)
7. No ripping clothes or pulling socks!
8. No saying, "Go away!"
9. No talking in church!
10. Keep my hands to myself!

I texted Mrs. L and let her know about his creation, and he placed it in his backpack for the next day at school. I believe there were times he referred to it for help at school, and I know there were days he referred to it for guidance after making a poor choice at home. The good choices book remained in his backpack all year, eventually an "out of sight" reminder. There are days where he tells me, "I don't need a good choices book anymore, I know what to do without it," and then there are days, like yesterday, when he made the wrong choice at school and needed a reminder.

I love making the consequences of behavior a conversation about our choices. A dear friend of mine, Kim Bird, introduced me to the disciplinary concept of "good choices" when our girls were toddlers. I heard her discussing a consequence for behavior with her then toddler in terms of good choices and poor choices, not bad ones. When I asked her about it, she explained making the disciplinary discussion about the choice the child made, versus making the child feel like they were "bad", changes the tone of the conversation. We used this technique with the older kids when they were young and have continued to use it with Matthew. It really resonated with him. It's ironic because life really is about choices and the consequences that follow those choices, no matter how old you are!

12

What Lies Ahead

The Costs of Autism

The latest studies estimate that 3.5 million Americans live with autism. Economic and medical experts estimate the lifetime autism-related costs range from $1.4 to $2.4 million dollars per individual, depending on whether there is a co-existing condition of intellectual disability. Families, insurance companies (that cover necessary services), and you (as taxpayers) share these costs of up to $236 billion dollars a year. And yet, that $236 billion dollars a year is simply not enough.

Autism is expensive on so many levels; there are lots of hidden costs. Obvious expenses include visits to developmental pediatricians, pediatric neurologists, pediatric psychiatrists, pediatric neuropsychologists, speech therapists, occupational therapists, physical therapists and applied behavioral analysis providers to name a few. Then there are the medications to control seizures and fine tune attention or quell anxiety. It is estimated that 25% of autistics are also epileptic. Medical specialists order tests, sometimes lots of them, to ensure seizures are under control or that vitamin levels remain stable. Some insurance companies cover autism-related expenses almost completely, while others enforce limits on number of visits or services allowed in a calendar year.

Educational expenses mount at the same time. Even if families live in districts with "good" public schools, many autistic students need outside help just to keep up and not fall behind their neuro-typical peers. Matthew spends extra hours each day after school and on the weekends trying to maintain grade level. I simply could not provide him all the support he needs and help my older kids with everyday life without outside help. Competent tutors or teachers require both time and treasure. Some parents must make the difficult choice between educational support and therapy. There aren't enough hours or dollars to go around.

Next up, hidden costs…autism camp in the summer, caregivers or babysitters (some autistics are not able to be left alone at any age), travel (choosing a trip and lodging that accommodates the needs of the family member on the spectrum), supports or reinforcers, lost income because a family member can't work due to caring for the autistic family member, and the list goes on. Hidden costs also include broken iPads, dry wall repair, eBay purchases of out of print books or videos, etc… Factor in saving, or trying to save, for the future. What if the autistic people we love are unable to find employment or care for themselves or continue receiving therapy after aging out of the system? Savings must be accumulated in the early years if at all possible.

All parents (hopefully) prepare for the day when they are no longer around to care for their children, but for parents of autistics this preparation is critical. Furthermore, plans need to exist in the event of tragedy, in the event of a parent or caregiver passing away prematurely: Are there adequate funds in place? Who is equipped to serve as a guardian? Will the autistic individual be able to continue his living and medical arrangements? It's a difficult, but necessary topic, Like I have mentioned, there must always be a Plan B.

Brett and I are very blessed; we have the necessary resources to meet Matthew's current needs and plan for his future. Many families are not as fortunate, and they have to make difficult economic decisions every day. These are economic decisions that can impede the access to early intervention and long-term progress. This financial quandary puts emotional stress on marriages, sometimes bringing couples closer, other times pushing them to a breaking point.

Once I realized how good our situation really was, I made a decision to try to help others who weren't as fortunate. I wanted to help the single moms and dads, working families or grandparents raising neuro-diverse kids without help or support. I wanted to help provide others with access to early intervention or a scholarship to attend Kids for Camp. I wanted to ease the load for someone who needed a hand. Volunteering with Autism Pensacola provides me the opportunity to make a difference in the lives of autistic individuals of all ages and their families. Through our annual Connecting the Pieces Gala in the spring and Steps For Autism walk in the fall, we raise funds to support Kids for Camp (a summer learning experience for children with autism and summer learning lab for educators and therapists), to provide emergency personnel with training, to provide educational and recreational activities for families affected by autism and so much more. My sincere hope is that my efforts, in some small way, pay forward the many gifts shared with me.

If You Know One Person With Autism...

The latest CDC statistics show that 1:68 children are on the spectrum, with the ratio being 1:42 for boys and 1:189 for girls.

One child with autism (photo credit: Mrs. Mommy, edited by Kim Bernstein)

As I looked at those statistics this morning, I thought it was kind of ironic, the whole 1 in... thing.Because that is kind of how this disorder or disease or spectrum works. An expression you hear repeatedly in the world of autism is "If you know one person with autism, you know one person with autism." I believe it is an expression that bears repeating and explanation. I think one (of the many) quandaries with autism is how it manifests so differently in each individual. Yes, commonalities exist, but the autism spectrum is vast and wide.

This phenomenon of how differently the disorder appears from one individual to the next further complicates this peculiar disorder. We do not know why or how someone gets autism. Is it genetic? Is it environmental? Is it auto-immune related? Is it driven by allergies to things like wheat and milk? Is it a combination of the above or something completely different? Why is it more prevalent in boys than girls? Is it really more prevalent in boys or does it present differently and more subtly in girls? The questions get more personal for a parent of an autistic.Could I have done something differently to prevent this for my child? Did I eat something during pregnancy that contributed? Did I let a virus or fever progress too far when Matthew was a baby before going to the doctor? In families with multiple children in which only one is affected, why that one? What was different? In families with multiple children in which more than one child is on the spectrum, while others are not, the questions are endless. At the end of the day, the why is one piece of the puzzle.

When you begin to look at autistic individuals and how different they are, more questions arise. Of course, there are similarities: delays in development, sensitivities to light and/or sounds, sensory issues, aversions to types of foods, desire for routine and structure, language impairment, etc. Yet these symptoms or nuances present so differently from person to person. Some autistics are non-verbal, while others speak. Some flap their hands, some sing aloud, others seek silence. Some seek physical touch and others withdraw from physical affection. Some like to play with trains, others bugs, others still musical instruments. Some autistics are intellectually gifted, while others are intellectually disabled.These gifts appear musical or artistic talents, in athletic abilities, in academic interests. These gifts can go undiscovered for years or present in early childhood.

When I think of the families I know affected by autism, I see preschoolers, elementary age kids, tweens, teens and young adults. I see individuals who use alternative forms of communication, ones with delayed or impaired language and others who speak appropriately for their age. Some work independently, others rely on help from family and government agencies. Their educational placements vary from inclusion settings to special education classes and homeschool to vocational training. So when you think about autism, do not limit your thoughts to stereotypes or tv portrayals like Rain Man or Max from Parenthood (though it is one of my favorite TV series of all time); think of Matthew, think of the autistic student in your child's class, think of whomever it is that you know or love with autism. Remember that just like each and every one of us, they want to be loved and accepted. Each and every one of us is different, but not less.

Plan B

Anyone who knows Brett or me very well knows that we are planners; good or bad, we are planners. We thrive knowing what is next, short-term and long-term. You also know that as parents, of neuro-typical or neuro-diverse children, plans change. Like it or not, it is necessary to have a Plan B.

If you had told me several years ago, in the midst of Matthew's diagnosis cycle, where he would be in school now and how well he would be performing, I must be honest—-I might not have believed you. I would have wanted to, but fear of failure, more mine than his, might have gotten in my way. Yet, the writings of people like Jess Wilson (Diary of a Mom) paved the way for me to believe and presume competence. Competence not just in Matthew, but in my abilities as a parent of a child with special needs. I never want to short change him. I do not want to close any doors or miss any opportunities, but I also do not want to set him up for failure. It is a balancing act.

We usually have two plans: A and B. Plan A: Matthew will finish his primary education with a diploma (on his own timetable) and pursue some type of secondary education; whether that is professional or vocational remains to be seen. Matthew will live independently and work in a job that he loves. If you ask him what he wants to be when he grows up, his first answer is usually "Matthew," which always makes me smile. He follows that up with something different almost every time from "fireman" to "mailman" to "doctor" to a

"Wiggle". We try to make educational decisions that don't prematurely close doors to any of those opportunities. Thus far, he continues to progress academically and works hard every day, just not always cheerfully like any other boy. We do not make these decisions or plans lightly. We involve his teachers, therapists, and medical professionals, and we pray for guidance and discernment. Then we make the most informed decisions we can.

Plan B: Matthew begins a vocational program instead of completing his diploma. Matthew lives either in an assisted living environment, group home, with Brett and I, or with one of his siblings during his adult years. He pursues his passion, whether that passion produces income or not, and he positively contributes to whatever community he lives in. Brett and I work with our financial advisor to plan for either scenario. We talk openly and honestly with our older children about their roles in Matthew's future. These discussions aren't always easy, but they are necessary.

Here's the thing though: this discussion, this process in general, applies to all four of our children, typical or diverse. Future planning, career planning, life planning can change at the drop of a hat, by tragedy or by choice. We want all of our children, including Matthew, to be the best versions of themselves possible. For them to achieve that "success," they must be involved and invested in the process This includes Matthew. We include him about conversations about school decisions, therapy, and other details of his life. We, as the parents, make the final decision, but we want Matthew to help make the plan.

What Keeps Me Up At Night

98% of the time, I live life half-full, always trying to find the good in situations, in people, life in general. Unfortunately, the other 2% of the time, usually at 2 a.m. when I cannot sleep, worry and "what if" take over. Sometimes I worry about ridiculous or irrational things, but the majority of time I worry about my children, their present and their future. For the older kids, it is teenage and young adult stuff: will they text and drive? Will they choose a career they are passionate about? Will they continue to practice their Catholic faith? Will they choose to live close to home? With Matthew, there are those same fears and countless others.

While I now work daily on presuming competence, there were times, when I as a "new" parent of an autistic child, know I talked about Matthew and autism in ways that could have been hurtful to him.

Since then, I read books like *NeuroTribes: The Legacy of Autism and the Future of Neurodiversity* by Steve Silberman and learned from the perspectives of adult autistics about things they heard as children and hear as adults and how hurtful those comments were (and are) to them. I learned that just because they might not be able to verbally communicate that they understand, they do. I want to make sure we openly communicate with Matthew about autism and the strengths and weaknesses that accompany it. I want him to know that he is autistic, like he is brown-eyed and brown haired. It does not define him, but is just part of what makes him Matthew.

I worry about making the right educational choices for him. Because of his expressive language delays, it is sometimes difficult to get a measure of what he comprehends at a given moment. I want to make sure that we explore every option for accessing his abilities. I want to make sure we do not underestimate his abilities, but I also want to make sure we do not place unrealistic expectations on him either. I want to ensure he is somewhere that will both challenge and nurture him for middle school, high school and college.

I anguish about friends. When you ask about his friends, he lists his siblings, Grand, and Ms. Robinson. When you push the question and ask about friends at school, he lists children in his class (Nathan, Darian, Kyle, Liam and Ben) and some children he is no longer in the class with, but sees at lunch or at recess (Natalie, Chad, Eleanor). He does not ask for playdates with those children. I hope it is because he is happy with the status quo. For the first time recently at a party, I noticed children looking at him and whispering. I do not think he noticed I pray he did not notice-but I did. I wanted to take the opportunity to educate the children, to tell them that he really is not so different from them, that he likes to play outside, that he likes to play games on the computer, that he is autistic. I wanted to explain what autism is and what it is not, but they were not children I knew and I did not know if I could find the words without tears.

Then there are even bigger worries, like what happens in the distant future. If he lives independently, will he be safe, will he be too trusting, will people take advantage of him? If he is unable to live independently, are we asking too much of our older children? Will their spouses and spouses' families and children love Matthew like we do? What if something happened to Brett or I now? How would that change the trajectory of his life and that of his siblings? I worry about Brett and how hard he works, so that I can plan and advocate. Then as quickly as the 2% comes, it goes. I am comforted by Matthew 6:34, "Therefore do not worry about tomorrow, for tomorrow will worry about itself. Each day has enough trouble of its own."

Hello!

Over the last year, Matthew began to ask to stay home alone on occasion. Usually, I was going somewhere he preferred not to go or he was engrossed in a video game or movie. After I got over the shock of his requests, I made a note to speak to his team about whether or not this was a realistic short-term (or long-term) goal and to seek advice about how to attain this goal. On our next round of visits, I polled his doctors and therapists and the overwhelming response was that yes, this is a reasonable goal. The "yes" was quickly followed by, "But you have to have a plan."

Several years ago, we disconnected our home phone line and now use my cell as our primary contact number. As a result, we no longer have a home phone. In order to "teach" Matthew to stay alone, we had to have a means of communication. We were not ready to give him a smart phone, not sure the flip phone made great sense either, and decided that the messaging systems on the computer and iPad were not exactly what we needed either. On the suggestion of a friend I made a trip to the Verizon store to check out the Gizmo Gadget watches for kids.

Gizmo Gadget watches are a watch, phone, messenger and video game all-in-one. The watch allows the administrator to set up the device to send and receive messages and call from 10 numbers. If the wearer does not answer after a certain number of rings, the caller can force the phone to pick up and hear what is occurring on the other end. Our version also has a tracking system (with a slight delay) in the event the wearer goes missing. Best of all, the monthly cost is $5, as opposed to the higher costs of a smart phone.

We purchased the Gizmo for Matthew for Christmas and taught him to use it while we were home. We "practiced" making and answering calls. He is so proud to have a "watch phone"! We decided to leave it with him anytime he is staying with a sitter (that I remember to leave it out and charged), so he can get used to making calls and answering calls. After a month of practice, Brett and I attended a birthday party and left Matthew with Walker. We decided this was a great time for Matthew to learn to use his Gizmo. We told Walker to give him lots of space and see how he did.

We were barely out of the driveway when he called my phone. You could hear the excitement and pride in his voice as he asked "Where are you going?" and "When will you be home?" As soon as he hung up with me, he called Brett. Same questions and same pride in his voice. We continued on to the party and were having a lovely time. About half an hour after we arrived at the party, we got texts and phone calls from the girls asking if Matthew was home alone. Apparently after calling Brett and me, Matthew called BethAnne and Peyton at college to tell them, "Mom and Dad are at a party!" He neglected to include that Walker was at home with him, so they were concerned he was home alone. After reassuring them that Matthew was not home alone, that this was practice, we had a good laugh. Both of the girls noticed that he actually talked to them when he called, more so than he sometimes does in person, so that was a bonus.

While he has progressed on his journey to independence, we are still not quite ready to leave him at home alone. We are continuing to practice and set the stage for future independence. We hope to reach that goal by the time Walker goes to college. Today, we practiced again and again he made phone calls as soon as I walked out the door. He called me and both of the girls. He likes the ability to reach out on his own. He has pride in his voice as he speaks. I am not sure if it is because he knows he is "growing" in his independence or if it is because he has a "watch phone," which is kind of like a spy gadget, or if he is just acting like the teenager that he is. Ultimately it does not matter why; it is one more step in his journey to independence.

A Butcher, a Baker or a Candlestick Maker

This past year Matthew developed a sense of understanding that college is not just a place you go after graduation; it is a place where you go to learn what you want to be when you grow up. He knows that BethAnne studies how to design buildings and houses and Peyton studies science so she can be a doctor, "like dad." He knows that Walker is looking for a college now too! He says he does not want Walker to go to college. (Me either; it's quiet and lonely with all of the big kids out of the house.)

All this college talk leads to questions about when Matthew will go to college, "Where will I go to college?" "Will I live in a tall house like Peyton? Can I take my iPad and my laptop and Buzz Lightyear to college?" All good, valid questions. Those questions are hard to answer. Yes, Matthew can go to college, maybe not in the traditional sense, but "college" none the less. As much as he likes to spend time with Grand and Mrs. Mommy, he might change his mind about moving away. PSC and UWF are excellent options locally.

College talk leads to job talk. Then the conversation gets more challenging. What is the right employment fit for Matthew? Autistic adults experience very high unemployment rates. I believe there is something he can do. We just have to identify that something. We have seen all he can accomplish when he sets his mind to it and when he is encouraged to persevere. If you ask him what he wants to be when he grows up, he says "a baker." He has obsessed over cakes for years now. It might be a realistic career goal for him. It does not require a degree. It can be performed in a variety of settings, from home-based to restaurant-based or a grocery bakery or even a stand-alone bakery.

Lately, I have been trying to include him more in the kitchen, to let him help me measure ingredients and stir, to get things from the refrigerator, and so on. We baked one of his birthday cakes in December and he chose the decorations and helped place them. I realize I have to encourage this interest and help him develop skills. Yes, it is a little scary introducing him to the kitchen and related equipment. However, if the future goal is independence in any measure, we have to start now. So, our summer experiment is going to be baking; we will let you know if we need tasters!

They Grow Up

Autism Pensacola initiated some new board committees this year. We hope to update our strategic plan and fine tune our mission with the findings. The three committees' efforts focus on Safety, Education and Adult Services. Matthew is fourteen, almost fifteen, and adulthood is upon us, so I volunteered for the Adult Services Committee. Our leader arranged for a meeting including two other parents of autistic children, our executive director, another board member, two medical students shadowing our organization and our Autism Works for the Community staff member. We talked about the issues facing adults with autism and they are vast: transportation, access to medical services, social life, employment, and housing, to name a few. We brainstormed about how our organization can better meet the needs of this community, how to spread our resources amongst this growing population without discontinuing services and how to fundraise for new programs.

The meeting brought out a lot of emotions, especially for the three of us with children on the spectrum. One of the other parents' child is already an adult, and they battle these issues daily. While they receive some services from other organizations, they are limited and hard to navigate. The other parents' child is nearer to adulthood than Matthew, and they are planning for his future. They have visited some amazing facilities in larger cities, but want to keep their child close to home. We all worry about what will happen when we are gone or no longer able to care for our children, and we worry about the responsibilities passed on to their siblings. We collectively want to do more for this segment of our population. We believe they are underserved.

Messaging is a challenge. Fundraising to help preschoolers is much simpler.

People want to help; their heartstrings are pulled by young children. The reality is that services have improved for children, early intervention is prevalent, more therapy providers are opening, public and private school options exist. Yet these autistic children grow up; they grow up into autistic adults. Yes, individuals learn how to cope better, they learn new skills and some may even achieve independence. Yet, for most the challenges do not disappear; they change, and they become more complicated. As the autistic individuals age, so do their caregivers, and with that comes more complications. . The statistics are staggering, 500,000 teens with autism will age into adulthood over the next decade and unemployment among adult autistics ranges from 75-85%, while the national unemployment rate hovers around 4%[8].

We have to tell the whole story of autism, not just the childhood version. We have to tell the stories of teenage sass, graduating not out of high school, but out of services, underemployment, unemployment, transportation challenges, lack of housing, APD wait lists, loss of caregivers and so on. We must remind ourselves and the rest of the world that autistic children do not grow out of autism; they grow up with autism, and we must provide an environment in which they can continue to grow and learn and thrive. I wish I had the answers. I do not, but I am sure that we as an organization, a community, a state, a nation, a world, we can do better. We must.

[8] Gerhardt, Peter F. "The Current State of Services for Adults with Autism." *Advancing Futures for Adults with Autism*, New York Center for Autism, Jan. 2009, afaa-us.org.

About the Author

Rocky Parra is a fifty year old wife, mom, retired CPA, dedicated volunteer, avid college sports and professional golf fan, and loves to visit old Catholic Churches. Rocky is passionate about advocating for Matthew and autism acceptance every chance she gets. In 2015, Rocky began writing about her family's experience with autism on her Facebook page. In 2018, she created Mrs. Mommy Reflects to further share Matthew's story.

Rocky and her husband, Brett, live in Pensacola, Florida with their four children, BethAnne, Peyton, Walker and Matthew.

You can find Rocky on instagram as @mrs__mommy or by email at MrsMommyWrites@gmail.com.

You can connect with me on:

f https://www.facebook.com/mrsmommyreflects

Printed in Great Britain
by Amazon

34300572R00088